CHAPELS

IN

ESSEX

Steeple Congregational chapel, 1857.

Back cover: Chingford Mount Congregational chapel, 1954.

CHAPELS IN ESSEX

Chapels and Meeting Houses in the
County of Essex, including Outer London

ROSALIND KAYE

Published by
Chellow Dean Press 1999

All profits from the sale of this book
will be donated to the Historic Chapels Trust

ISBN 0 9537549 0 1

Photographs by Rosalind Kaye
unless otherwise indicated.

Designed and typeset by Buffey & Buffey,
Coggeshall, Essex

Repro by Facsimile Graphics,
Coggeshall, Essex

Printed in Great Britain
by Mayland Graphics, Essex

ACKNOWLEDGEMENTS

My thanks go to the following people who responded generously to the request for information about individual chapels, and without whom the work would not have been completed:

R. Alford, O. Allen, T. Andrews, A. Asplin, P. Baker, A. Baldwin, G. Barber, G. Barker, R. Barratt, R. Bazett, B. Beard, C. Bird, S. Boniface, F. Brereton, A. Brining, A. Brooks, G. Brown, G. Brown, P. Brown, D. Carter, M. Clark, P. Clark, J. Copsey, A. Corder-Birch, M. Cowling, M. Cross, P. Croxton-Smith, L. Curtis, M. Dalley, S. Deacon, J. Denniss, D. Doo, D. Doran, J. Drury, M. Fisher, M. Ford, M. Ford, L. Francis, T. Gallifent, M. Gould, D. Greasley, B. Grinham, E. Healey, J. Hogg, A. Hooper, A. Hurren, R. Jiggins, N. Knowles, M. Langstone, J. Lee, B. Lewis, D. McConnell, R. McDougall, I. McMaster, B. & A. Mayo, R. Meloy, C. Mensah, O. Moffatt, D. Norman, D. Oates, A. Parker, J. Pease, E. Phelps, D. Poynter, A. Rowing, C. Rowles, P. Ryan, F. Sainsbury, T. Searle, A. Smith, H. Spyve, R. Strutt, F. Trotter, M. Turner, P. Turner, R. Walker, P. Watkinson, A. Weedon, A. West, A. Whitbread, J. White, A. Whyte, M. Williamson, R. Wilson, G. Wire, A. Woodley.

My thanks go to the many people who welcomed me into their chapels and allowed me to take photographs there. I am grateful to those who readily agreed to the inclusion of illustrations of interiors in the book.

I would also like to thank: the staff of the Essex Record Office and Local Studies Library for their efficient services; Dr Janet Cooper for sharing information from current research; Janet Ede, Norma Virgoe and Tom Williamson for sharing their experience of recording chapels; and Jean Aberdour (dec) for contacting the Essex Parish Recorders.

I am indebted to Dr Philip Hills, Robert Hurley, Elizabeth Watthews and my sister Dr Elaine Kaye for their encouragement and helpful criticism.

INTRODUCTION

The study of religious architecture until recently concentrated on Anglican churches, but has now broadened to include nonconformist places of worship, allowing a better understanding of the whole.[1] The loss of chapels through closure and demolition, and the modernisation of interiors, has given urgency to the study of those which remain. Few were designed by major architects, but they symbolise the struggle for freedom of conscience and thought, and as such are part of our culture.

Essex has always been strongly nonconformist, having had in the eighteenth century one of the highest proportions of Independents in the country.[2] The particular geography and development of the county, which includes outer London, seaside resorts, towns and rural areas, have contributed to its distinctive distribution of chapels; Congregationalist were spread throughout, Methodists were concentrated in the north-east corner and outer London, with Baptists in the towns and seaside areas. The growth of Southend and outer London coincided with the peak years of nonconformist membership while the post-war new towns of Basildon and Harlow developed at a time of diminishing congregations.

This study considers the major nonconformist denominations. Of the smaller sects, the Peculiar People have been included as they are almost unique to Essex. The differences between the buildings of each, apart from Quakers, are small compared with their similarities so they are considered together. The study provides an overview of the architectural development. With some eight hundred chapels, past and present, it has only been possible to mention some of the buildings in the text; details of dates and present usage have been confined to the Directory.

The Friends Meeting House in Colchester was converted from a Georgian house in 1971-74; a hexagonal Meeting Room was added behind, overlooking the garden.
Reproduced by courtesy of the artist, Tim Holding.

ORIGINS

The roots of religious dissent can be traced back to the sixteenth century. Following the Reformation, the Puritans felt the changes had not gone far enough; they wished to purify the Church of much of the surviving ritual while the Separatists preferred to dispense with all set forms of worship. In Essex Puritan activity centred in the north around Dedham and Colchester, and also Maldon.

Puritanism was fostered by the county's proximity to Cambridge; at the University, Emmanuel College, founded by Mildmay to train preaching ministers, and Sidney Sussex with a similar purpose, provided an ample supply of Puritan clergy. Sympathetic patrons looked to Cambridge for their appointments; notable among these was the Earl of Warwick with some twenty livings in his gift.[3]

The Presbyterian Church established during the Interregnum gained the support of many in Essex. Those with more extreme views, the Independents, probably felt able to express their views more openly in Parliamentary Essex, well away from the Royalist front lines, than in other parts of the country. Both groups took encouragement from the Declaration of Breda, 1660, in which Charles II expressed his readiness to grant his subjects 'a liberty to tender consciences' in matters of religion not affecting the peace of the realm.

All hope was lost when the Act of Uniformity was passed by the newly elected Royalist Parliament in 1662, which required clergy to accept the Book of Common Prayer, with ordination by bishops, and renounce opposition to the King. Those unable to accept these conditions were ejected from their livings on St Bartholomew's Day, 24 August 1662. During the period 1660 - 62 some 2000 clergy, lecturers and fellows were deprived of their posts in England and Wales, more than 100 of these in Essex.[4] Quakers, having no clergy, did not suffer ejectment but were subject to the same ban on gathering for worship outside the Church.

Many congregations followed their ejected clergy to gather for worship in secret, risking prosecution, despite the various Acts of the Clarendon Code which were designed to suppress Dissent. Nineteen present-day congregations in Essex can trace their origins to 1662 or earlier. A plaque in the porch of Christchurch, Coggeshall, pays tribute to John Owen, one-time Vicar of Coggeshall and a leading Independent, through whose teaching the congregation left the Church to found Coggeshall Independent chapel.

Under the Declaration of Indulgence, 1672, clergy and meeting places could be licensed for dissenting worship and more than fifty ejected clergy in Essex took advantage of this freedom.[5] Most licensed their own houses, few of which can be located today. However, a plaque outside a building in Billericay High Street records that Independents worshipped there in 1672, and Wood Hall, Arkesdon, another licensed house, is still identified on the map.

Quakers had been active in Essex following the death in Colchester Castle of James Parnell, the young Quaker preacher. In 1667 George Fox visited Halstead and helped to form six Monthly Meetings, five of them in the north of the county. 'Apart from the ever reckless Quakers, who throughout the reign of Charles II had built their own Meeting Houses, and had rebuilt them when they were pulled down, few

Dissenting congregations had deemed it wise to advertise their presence to would-be persecutors by constructing their own places of worship.'[6] Only the meeting house at Stebbing survives from that time, being the oldest purpose-built place of nonconformist worship in Essex.

Following the Glorious Revolution of 1688, the Act of Toleration, 1689, provided freedom of worship for non-episcopal trinitarian Christians, and thus institutionalised Dissent. Immediately buildings were licensed for worship - a house, a barn or a room at an inn - and congregations met openly. However Dissenters were subject to civil disabilities which lasted into the nineteenth century.

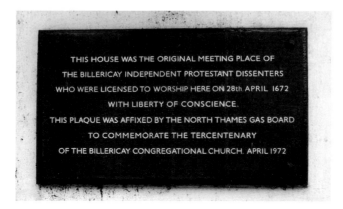

Few of the houses licensed for worship in 1672 can be identified today but this plaque in Billericay High Street marks the building where the Independents worshipped at that time.

EARLY MEETING HOUSES
Toleration to 1800

The Independent Meeting House at Bocking End, built in 1707 and considerably altered a century later.

Within a very few years of Toleration congregations began to erect purpose-built chapels, among the first being Saffron Walden and Colchester Independents. Most of the earliest Meeting Houses in Essex have been replaced over the years and those which survive have been considerably altered, but contemporary drawings and descriptions remain.

Meeting Houses of this period had the charm and simplicity of domestic buildings of the time, reflecting the simplicity of the style of worship. With a reluctance to sell good land to Dissenters, they were often built on 'back land'. This had the advantage of being inconspicuous at a time of continuing political uncertainty; it was also less expensive, an important consideration for Dissenters who were obliged to pay Church Rates in addition to funding their own buildings.

The style and materials were local. A simple rectangle with two doors on the long-wall

Drawing of the long-wall facade of Stansted Old Meeting, erected in 1698.
Reproduced by courtesy of Essex Record Office.

facade was the usual plan. A hipped roof with pantiles, common in East Anglia, is to be found in the north of the county, for example at Foxearth Independent while Saffron Walden General Baptist, being larger, had a double roof supported inside by pillars.

The focal point of worship was the preaching of the Word, rather than the celebration of the Eucharist, and this was given expression in the internal arrangements. The pulpit on the long wall opposite the doors was surrounded on three sides by pews, allowing everyone to both

The first chapel at Castle Hedingham, built in 1719. The double roof was supported by pillars inside. The drawing was made by Sarah Hubbard in 1842, just as it was about to be pulled down.
Reproduced by courtesy of Castle Hedingham United Reformed Church.

see and hear the preacher. Two side aisles gave access to the pews from the doors, and a gallery provided additional seating. The Independent Meeting House at Witham was recalled from the late eighteenth century:

> There were side and front galleries, a high pulpit with a narrow entrance, over which was suspended a large round sounding board, and in front, close under the pulpit, the clerk's reading desk. In the gallery opposite the pulpit was the singers' oblong pew, with a raised table along the middle; its occupants ranged from 20 to 30, including instrumentalists, who manipulated a flute, clarionette, bassoon, and bass viol. The "Table Pew" was in the middle of the chapel, close under the clerk's desk. At one time during the dispensation of the Lord's Supper not only the pastor and deacons, but all the communicants gathered in this pew. …The table pew at other times afforded free sittings to the aged poor of the church.[7]

This early internal arrangement does not survive in Essex but may still be seen at Walpole Independent chapel in Suffolk, now in the care of the Historic Chapels Trust.

Quaker Meeting Houses differed as there were no professional clergy. A raised bench along one wall, for those responsible for the worship, faced benches in an open square for the members of the meeting. At Stebbing there was

> a moveable screen, separating, when required, the men's and women's meeting... The doorway, on the north side, has a massive oak bar for fastening from the inside, suggestive of the times when the violence of intruders was feared.[8]

Between 1715 and 1718, in the still uncertain political climate, a committee of London ministers carried out a survey of Dissenting congregations in England and Wales. The Evans List, as it is known, records twenty two Presbyterian, thirteen Independent and seven Baptist congregations in Essex. (The list does not include Quakers.) Half of these were situated in Boroughs or Market towns and a further quarter in the area of the wool trade in the north of the county.[9]

The General Baptist chapel of 1729, Saffron Waldon, now in commercial use.

The Independent chapel, Colchester, built in 1766. The octagonal shape is echoed in the present Lion Walk United Reformed chapel.
Reproduced by courtesy of Essex Record Office.

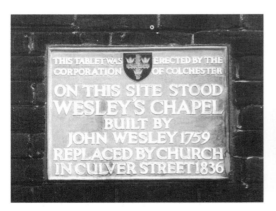

Wesley's chapel stood near the present Castle Methodist chapel in Colchester.

Potter Street Particular Baptist chapel, Harlow, has a fine doorway.

GEORGIAN PERIOD
1780-1840

After the rapid expansion in building following Toleration, very few chapels were erected during the fifty years to 1780. The Evangelical Revival, originating within the Church of England, also influenced the Baptists and Independents. John Wesley made more than twenty visits to Colchester, preaching first in homes and later in the new Meeting House.[10] Priority was given to gaining converts and establishing worshipping groups but from 1800 chapel-building resumed in Essex.

John Wesley was influential in architecture as well as in spiritual matters. For a period he had recommended an octagonal plan, or if that was not feasible, a rectangle with the proportions twenty-one to eighteen. These provided greater capacity for a given wall space, were easy to heat and light, and had good acoustics. The almost-square plan continued in use into the 1820s and may be seen in the Particular Baptist chapels at Thorpe-le-Soken and Harwich, in the Independent chapel at Manningtree, with its elegant curved sash windows, and in the Wesleyan chapel at Great Oakley.

The more lasting influence came from Wesley's City Road chapel of 1778, together with the decision of Conference in 1790 that all Wesleyan chapels should be built to this design (or that of the smaller one in Bristol). The plan

A 'square' chapel in Harwich, now used as a workshop. Ebenezer was built by the Wesleyan Methodists and sold later to the Strict Baptists.
Reproduced by courtesy of Essex County Newspapers.

owed much to contemporary Anglican buildings which took the form of a rectangular auditory with no marked distinction between nave and chancel, a gallery and central pulpit. Wesley died in 1791 and without his strong

The quietly restrained Friends Meeting House, Dunmow, built in 1833.

leadership differences began to surface. The architectural recommendations were applied more freely; nevertheless the longways rectangular plan became universal in non-conformity for nearly a century. As chapels were enlarged or refurbished, the pulpit and pews were reordered in the longways arrangement.[11]

The Independents, already the most numerous in the county, added more than forty chapels to their number during this period and were to be found throughout, with the exception of inland Tendring Hundred. Baptists were expanding, but more slowly; in the London area they were concentrated south

of the Thames, which may account for their later spread into metropolitan Essex. All the General Baptists had turned to Calvinism, joining the Particular Baptists by the end of this period.

The 1820s saw a great increase in Wesleyan chapels, concentrated in Tendring Hundred and, to a lesser extent, in the metropolitan area. Methodism has been able to flourish where Old Dissent was weak, as in the north-east corner of the county, but with Independents well established through the rest of the county, Wesleyans found it more difficult to gain a footing there.[12]

The Congregational chapel of 1841 at West Mersea. The porch was a recent addition to the 'square' building.

CLASSICAL
1800-1870

By 1800 nearly all civic buildings took the classical form. The architectural section of the Congregational Year Book of 1847 noted that 'The improvement in public taste which has been seen in our national edifices and private habitations, during the last twenty-five years, has at length reached the meeting-houses of Nonconformist...'.[13] Most of the chapels illustrated that year took the classical form with pedimented gable end and pilasters or pillared portico.

Nonconformists had been challenging their exclusion from participation in government and in 1828 the Test Act was repealed, thus allowing them to hold civic office; their increasing confidence within society and their sense of civic pride were being expressed in their buildings.

Manningtree Wesleyan chapel was one of the first to adopt the classical style, even before Wesley's City Road chapel acquired its Doric

The Independent chapel at Saffron Walden built in 1811 in the classical style, with broken pediment and Ionic columned porch.

James Fenton designed the Independent chapel at Braintree in 1832, using the classical style.

porch in 1809. The Particular Baptist chapels at Eld Lane, Colchester and Salem, Romford, and the Quaker Meeting House in Duke Street, Chelmsford, are later examples, while the Congregational chapels at Maldon, Upminster and Stockwell Street, Colchester, were all refronted in this style. While most looked to Greece for inspiration, a minority chose the Romanesque, such as the Congregational chapels at Dunmow, Stansted and Tollesbury.

In 1859, as Spurgeon laid the foundation stone of the Tabernacle in London, he declared 'Every Baptist place should be Grecian, never Gothic.' Greek and Hebrew were sacred languages and 'Greek is the Baptist's tongue'.[14] While his words were not strictly followed in Essex, Baptists did not embrace the Gothic style to the same extent as did other denominations.

Interiors did not follow the classical style, with the elaborate decoration to be seen in public buildings, but remained simple. They were now being arranged in the longways plan with pulpit and doors facing each other on the shorter sides. Box pews of the period may still be seen at Castle Hedingham Congregational and Ashdon Particular Baptist chapels, while in a few other places they remain only in the gallery.

The imposing Friends Meeting House in Duke Street, Chelmsford, spoke of the standing of Quakers in the town at the time.

The Congregational chapels at Maldon (left) and Stockwell Street, Colchester (right), were each refronted in the classical style.

Chigwell Row Congregational chapel, 1804.

GOTHIC REVIVAL
1830-1930

James Fenton was probably the first to adopt the Gothic style for chapels in Essex. His Independent chapel at Billericay in austere Early English was built in 1838.

Under the influence of the Oxford Movement, Anglicans reintroduced the ceremonial expression of worship, and adopted the Gothic style of building which suited the new liturgy. The writer of the Congregational Year Book of 1847 observed that 'a taste for the English style is now cultivated by non-conformists themselves'. He favoured the Gothic style because of its beauty and flexibility, and, above all, its moderate cost.[15] Within a very few years the new chapels illustrated in the Year Books were predominantly Gothic in style.

However the changes in nonconformist architecture sprang from fashion, social confidence and expense rather than any new thinking in liturgy.

Estimates for chapels in both classical and Gothic styles showed the latter to be less expensive. If objections to Gothic proved insuperable the Roman style was available, but if money was to be spent in the service of God it should be used with 'taste and judgement, so as to attract, rather than repel persons of intelligence and respectability.'[16]

The Congregational chapel at Orsett, 1843, in Early English.

Jobson, writing particularly for Wesleyans, asserted more definitely that Gothic was the style of choice for chapels, though not in every detail. It grew out of Christian worship and was seen immediately as ecclesiastical; also its steep roof suited English weather. He argued that Methodists, as a united Society, should agree a common style; in this they had an advantage over the Congregationalists (whose chapels maintained their independence). With no Government grants, Queen Anne's Bounty or landed property to support repairs, Methodists should choose the cheaper style.[17]

In Essex, while the majority of Methodists followed Jobson's advice, Congregationalists reflected the national 'battle of styles', erecting both classical and Gothic chapels throughout the middle years of the century with Gothic eventually predominating.

Being a cheaper style, Gothic appeared first in provincial towns while the more expensive classical style lingered in the metropolitan area until the 1880s. An austere Early English style was seen first in the Congregational chapels at Billericay, Halstead High Street and Ingatestone. Decorated Gothic was widely used and may be seen in the Congregational chapels at Cranbrook, Ilford, and Hatfield Heath; also in Southend at Crowstone and Westcliff. Perpendicular was used at Goodmayes Wesleyan and Walthamstow Central Baptist chapels.

Nonconformists rarely followed the Gothic in every historic detail but rather employed a free interpretation of the style. Chapels were almost universally built end-on to the road, so greater attention was paid to the facade; an otherwise simple building might have an elaborate Gothic facade, as may be seen in the Wesleyan chapels at Dovercourt and Frinton.

Notable among the critics of the style was J. A. Tabor, a deacon of Lion Walk

Congregational, Colchester. As his chapel was being rebuilt in the Gothic he issued a pamphlet protesting against 'the unchristian and unseemly innovations' and 'the vainglorious erection, for the worship of God, of highly architectural and gorgeous edifices, with massive towers and lofty and defiant spires.' (Lion Walk had, then, the tallest spire in town.) He pointed to the secular and political attitudes, as well as the worldly and sectarian rivalry involved in the choice of architecture, reminding his readers that 'the temple of God is a humble and contrite heart.'[18]

Despite objections the Gothic style in non-conformist hands expanded into transept, apse and tower towards the end of the century, little different in plan from Churches of the Oxford Movement. However the internal arrangement of central pulpit with communion table below, pews with side aisles, and gallery, remained though not well suited to the shape of the building. The organ, introduced mid-century, was often placed at the back, in the gallery (the traditional place for musicians). Later it might occupy an apse behind the pulpit, together with the choir; below were vestries and, in Baptist chapels, changing rooms for candidates with convenient access to the baptistry in front of the pulpit.

Some chapels included a chancel. For architectural reasons the pulpit was placed to one side, while the communion table, organ and choir occupied the chancel. (Towards the end of the century an attempt was made to introduce a more formal liturgy which gave equal emphasis to sacraments and preaching. Chapels in this movement placed the pulpit to one side for liturgical reasons.)

The comfort of the congregation was being considered in the latter part of the century. Trinity Congregational, Walthamstow, provided cushioned pews in its new building in 1871.

Later in the nineteenth century Decorated Gothic was used, as here at Halstead. Barnes of Ipswich designed the Parsonage Lane Congregational chapel in 1875.

While two aisles were retained, a single outer door was often adopted leading to a lobby; from there doors left and right led into the sanctuary, thus reducing draughts. Various heating, lighting and ventilation devices were described in the architectural sections of the Baptist Handbooks and Congregational Year Books, such as Tortoise stoves at Maldon Baptist in 1897, a Constantine convoluted stove at Romford Congregational in 1877 and an Archimedean exhaust for ventilation at Ray Lodge Congregational in 1901.

Towards the end of the nineteenth century, the last of the discriminatory Acts having been repealed, nonconformists were playing a full part in society. As the seaside towns and new areas of metropolitan Essex were being developed, they were able to secure prominent sites for their chapels; in Clacton-on-Sea, Trinity Wesleyan, Pier Avenue Baptist and Christchurch Congregational chapels are each main-street features in the town, while Forest Gate Congregational occupies a commanding position in Romford Road. In Southend Gothic

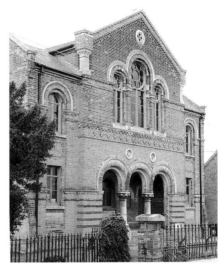

Gothic was not acceptable to everyone, being associated in some people's minds with 'popery'. At Dunmow the Congregationalists chose Romanesque for their 1869 chapel.

continued to be chosen until about 1930, although from the turn of the century an increasing variety of styles began to appear elsewhere.

Alone among nonconformists, the Quakers remained untouched by the Gothic revival. Their buildings during this period retained a modest Georgian appearance in most cases, with the interior arrangement unchanged. The denomination had resisted the Evangelical Revival and lost members until the middle of the century; it had not seen the great expansion in building of the other denominations.

The Congregational chapel at Hatfield Heath for which Lewis Banks employed the Decorated style in 1865.

VILLAGE CHAPELS AND TIN TABERNACLES

While the Gothic style was more economical than its predecessor, it nonetheless required a considerable sum of money to achieve. Many small congregations and communities could not aspire to anything architectural yet managed to build one, two, three or - as in Tillingham - four places of worship. Most were simple rectangular structures with a single door and plain windows, possibly edged with coloured glass. As the debt was paid off or money became available, a porch might be added to reduce draughts, or a room for meetings or Sunday School.

Primitive Methodist chapels in rural areas, such as this at Langley, were built on a modest scale, most of their members being agricultural labourers.

The simple charm of the Peculiar People's chapel at Tillingham.

The small size would not allow for two aisles so a single aisle led from door to communion table and pulpit. A portable organ, such as that at Kirby Cross Primitive Methodist chapel, with its mouse-proof pedals, might provide music, while heating came from a stove. The Congregational chapel at Woodham Ferrers is thought to have had one of the first tortoise stoves made at Colne Valley Iron Works in Halstead.[19] Hat pegs round the walls and a text painted on the wall over the pulpit were common, and survived until recently at Crockleford Primitive Methodist chapel.

The iron chapel or 'tin tabernacle' at Old Heath, Colchester still serves its congregation.

Dunmow Strict Baptist, Chappel Congregational and Thorpe-le-Soken Primitive Methodist are among the remaining small village chapels but many cannot be sustained with dwindling congregations and have sadly closed.

An economic alternative to bricks and mortar was a prefabricated iron chapel or 'tin tabernacle' as they were affectionately known. The first examples of such buildings were displayed at the Great Exhibition of 1851 and catalogues of halls, hospitals, churches and chapels were available throughout the second half of the century. With their timber frames and inner wooden walls, they made serviceable and homely places of worship.

Many congregations in both towns and villages began meeting in a hired room, then purchased an iron building. If the cause grew a permanent building would be erected and the iron chapel either retained as a hall or dismantled and sold. Some were never replaced and continue to serve their congregations, among them Chignal St James Baptist and Old Heath Congregational chapels.

Two kinds of brick used decoratively at Clavering Primitive Methodist chapel.

A typical village chapel at Horndon-on-the-Hill.

The Congregational chapel at Roydon, 1851.

The Peculiar People's chapel at Corringham, 1914.

HALLS AND SUNDAY SCHOOLS

The first Sunday Schools in the late eighteenth century were interdenominational but during the nineteenth century they became increasingly the preserve of the nonconformists. Once a chapel was established, a schoolroom might be added, and in some cases also used as a day school.

In the second half of the nineteenth century strict Calvinism gave way to a more universal view of salvation. Inner convictions were expressed in social 'good works' and congregations busied themselves with a variety of week-night activities such as bazaars, lectures and teas in an effort to preserve the chapel community in competition with neighbouring chapels. Lecture Halls, Institutes, Schoolrooms and Parlours were added to chapels in great numbers, often in matching architectural style. Upton Park Primitive Methodists added a Church Parlour, and Sunday School with Lecture Hall, to their chapel, the inscriptions over the door still being visible. Stockwell Street Congregational, Colchester, added the 'Sabbath Schools' in 1867.

Methodists, hoping to attract members in urban areas, built Central Halls which offered worship and social activities in a less formal setting. Lloyd Park Central Hall, Walthamstow, has the appearance of a civic, rather than ecclesiastical building.

The signs above the doors indicate that the Primitive Methodists at Plashet Grove, Newham, had facilities for many kinds of activity.

Sunday Schools were added to chapels to accommodate the children's classes and week-night activities, as at Headgate Congregational, Colchester (below), and Rayleigh Wesleyan Methodist chapels (above) (the latter bought by the Salvation Army when the Methodists moved from the High Street).

EARLY TWENTIETH CENTURY
1900-1940

In a dramatic break from the Gothic style, Morley Horder designed the Congregational chapel at Leyton in 1899 with plain mullioned windows and a deep tiled roof.

The Edwardian period saw a new freedom of expression in many aspects of life. The Arts and Crafts movement had been challenging traditional Victorian taste and methods of production, while fresh inspiration in architecture came from Mackintosh, Lutyens, Voysey and others. When the Fetter Lane congregation moved to join with Leyton Congregational they employed Morley Horder, an architect of the new school, to design their building. The massive shape with rows of unadorned mullioned windows and deep tiled

William Hayne designed Hutton Mount Union chapel in 1913 to blend into the wooded area surrounding it.

roof was quite unlike any of its predecessors; surprising, too, must have been the classical interpretation of the 'auditory' inside.

Three years later Woodford Green Union chapel employed Harrison Townsend, best known for his Art Galleries, to design their new building. The exterior had little to suggest that it was used for worship, but inside the architect drew on Byzantine features to create a large, well-lit open space; arches built from specially made thin local brick support the roof and, originally, a small dome. The Baptist chapels at Pier

Avenue, Clacton and West Ham Central Mission also drew on the same architectural style.

Another style to be adopted in the early years of the century was the Art Nouveau. The Baptist chapels at Victoria Road South, Chelmsford and Frinton each use this for their interior decoration, in wood and glass.

Many chapels built during this period use brick, wood and tile in a way which suggests the influence of the Domestic style - deep hipped tiled roofs, brick walls and wooden doors and window frames - as for example at

Brentwood Baptist, Hutton Mount Union and Holland-on-Sea first Wesleyan chapels.

Larger buildings enhanced the position of the preacher by arranging the pews in an arc, sometimes with radial aisles, so that everyone faced the pulpit directly. The effect was further emphasised by a raked floor. The Baptist chapels at Frinton and Ilford, together with Cranbrook and Chingford Congregational chapels were designed with these features.

Chapel-going reached its peak at the turn of the century and diminished throughout this period. The Congregational Year Books note a number of buildings designed so as to allow for expansion if required, hinting at doubts about the future. Plans were also made for a variety of uses; at Hornchurch Congregational the pulpit could be removed for concerts while at Goodmayes Congregational plans were designed to suit 'all forms of entertainments'. The Union of Primitive, Wesleyan and United Methodists in 1932 afforded the Methodist Church the opportunity to reduce the number of chapels as nearby congregations amalgamated; Bradfield Primitive, Grays United and Writtle Wesleyan Methodist chapels were among those which became redundant at this time.

A typical between-the-wars chapel, the Wesleyan Methodist at Hadleigh.

The compact Congregational chapel at Danbury, 1937.

The Friends Meeting House at Stebbing, now in community use. Built in 1674, it is the oldest surviving purpose-built nonconformist place of worship in Essex.

The Presbyterian Meeting House, Little Baddow, built in 1707.

The Independent chapel, Coggeshall, 1710. It has been extended and altered several times.

The Friends Meeting House at Earls Colne. A Meeting House was built on the site in 1674 but there is evidence to suggest that it was rebuilt in 1733. The smaller building was added in 1986.

The Independent chapel at Terling opened in 1753.

The Particular Baptist chapel, Thorpe-le-Soken, built in 1802. A 'square' chapel with pyramid roof.

The Independent chapel, Castle Hedingham. Built in the classical style in 1842, it retains two entrances.

The Gothic tower of Buckhurst Hill Congregational chapel, 1873. The body of the chapel was replaced in 1955.

Brightlingsea Wesleyan Methodist Chapel, 1843.

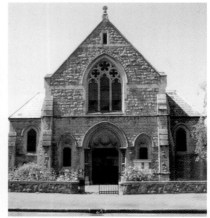

The Wesleyan Methodist chapel of 1863 at Elmstead Market with matching Sunday School. The chapel is being replaced.

The Wesleyan Methodist chapel at Hermon Hill, Redbridge, built in 1876.

During most of the nineteenth century chapels were designed with a simple rectangular plan. The high central pulpit, with communion table below, faced the central area of pews, as here at St Osyth Wesleyan Methodist chapel, 1855.

Towards the end of the century larger chapels were planned with an apse behind the pulpit to house the organ, as here at the Wesleyan Methodist chapel, Romford, built in 1887.

In the early twentieth century the chancel contained the organ, communion table and often the choir; the high pulpit was placed to one side. Here at Frinton Free chapel, the floor is raked and pews arranged in an arc.

Post-war, the communion table takes the central position with the pulpit placed to one side of the dais, as preaching and the sacraments are given equal emphasis in the liturgy. Theydon Bois Baptist chapel, 1962.

The hammer and trowel used in the ceremony of laying the foundation stone of Little Oakley Methodist chapel, 1969.

Pew number and name-card holder which enabled rented pews to be identified. The small metal ring holds an individual communion cup. Frinton Free chapel.

Corbel at Christchurch Congregational chapel, Clacton-on-Sea. Each one in the chapel and halls is different.

Art nouveau decorative detail designed by William Hayne, at Victoria Road South Baptist chapel, Chelmsford.

Art nouveau decorative detail designed by William Hayne, at Frinton Free chapel.

The baptistry at Pier Avenue Baptist chapel, Clacton-on-Sea. In most Baptist chapels the baptistry is covered by the dais when not in use.

Texts were often painted on the wall, though few survive today; this at Great Bromley Wesleyan Methodist chapel, now closed.

Carved pew end and umbrella stand, Bradfield Wesleyan Methodist chapel. The pews came from Culver Street Wesleyan Methodist chapel, Colchester, which was replaced in 1970.

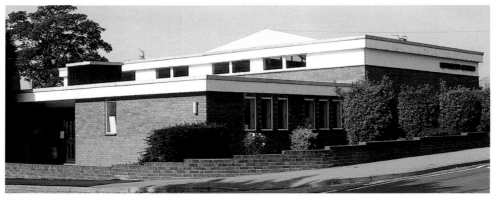

The Methodist chapel at Waltham Abbey, built in 1975. The worship area and other rooms are included in a single complex.

The Baptist chapel at North Springfield, Chelmsford, built in 1982 to serve the new area of housing.

Redundant chapels make comfortable homes.

POST WAR
1945 ONWARDS

Metropolitan Essex suffered considerable damage and destruction during the war which provided congregations and denominations with an opportunity to review the siting of their buildings. Chapels with a viable congregation were repaired or replaced. Others located in areas which had changed in nature, for example become industrialised, 'ported' their war damage compensation to fund new chapels in recently developed areas in need of provision. Thus the new Baptist chapels at Claybury Park and Marks Gate received contributions from Bow Road while Aveley Methodist was funded from Charles Street Primitive Methodist. Areas which were becoming multi-faith saw a steep decline in chapel-going; Methodists addressed this by amalgamating groups of congregations to form Kier Hardie and Forest Gate chapels.

The new towns of Basildon and Harlow, formed to accommodate London overspill, were planned with community facilities, including places of worship, and non-conformists took this opportunity to found congregations and eventually build chapels.

By the 1960s postwar restrictions had eased. A number of chapels replaced older buildings in a modern style such as the Baptists at Theydon Bois, the Congregationalists at South Ockendon and the Methodists at Manor Park and Holland-on-Sea.

After the war the recognisable 'chapel' shape was still being used, as at Rainham Methodist (1959), Upminster (1959) and Becontree (1964) Baptist chapels. (Top, middle and bottom.)

More recent chapels have included their halls and other facilities in a single complex, for example Cann Hall and Colchester Methodists and Leytonstone Union. The vocabulary of buildings changed most noticeably during this period. No longer is there a common chapel style, immediately recognisable as such, as in the Victorian era; but for the notice-board, many post-war chapels could, from their appearance, be a library, civic hall or school.

A change in liturgy, giving equal emphasis to the sacraments and preaching, has been expressed in the internal arrangements; the pulpit has been lowered and moved to one side leaving the communion table in the central position. A lectern or musical instruments may also occupy the dais. Chairs provide greater comfort and flexibility than pews, allowing the sanctuary to be used for a variety of purposes in addition to Sunday worship. With diminishing congregations, some seating becomes redundant; at Great Oakley Methodist the gallery has been isolated by a false ceiling, making the heating more efficient while at Walton-on-the-Naze the space below the end gallery has been screened to make a place for gatherings.

New chapels have brought new ideas too. At Plume Avenue URC, Colchester, the creche is within sight (but not sound) of the congregation, while Holland-on-Sea Methodist is arranged diagonally with the communion table in one corner lit by a high window in the roof extension. Two congregations with valuable town-centre sites - Hornchurch Baptist and Lion Walk URC, Colchester - have been rebuilt with shops on the ground floor and worship area upstairs, thus ensuring both a visible presence in the town and a continuing source of income. New building materials have also offered new possibilities, such as the Swedish timber portal frames used at Thorpe Bay and Loughton Methodists.

Basildon Strict Baptist (1953), the first chapel to be built in the New Town.

From the nineteen seventies chapels and their additional rooms were being designed as a single complex, not immediately recognisable as a place of worship, as at Romford (1974) and Cann Hall (1992) Methodist chapels. (Top and bottom.)

New materials became available, such as the Swedish portal frames, used here to form arches to support the roof of Thorpe Bay Methodist chapel, Southend (1995).

FOUNDATION STONES

On entering a chapel one may pause to read an inscription recording that the minister or representative of the Women's Guild, perhaps, had laid the foundation stone on a certain date. From the nineteenth century it was customary to mark the rising building with a ceremony, usually followed by a meeting, meal and collection for the building fund.

The choice of stone-layer depended on circumstances. A new congregation erecting its first building might call on benefactors or representatives of nearby congregations who had helped to establish the chapel, while a congregation replacing its building would choose representatives of groups within the chapel such as Deacons or Sunday School. Some stones commemorated the lives of individuals who had been members of the congregation. Initialled bricks were also sold and incorporated into the fabric.

Towards the end of the nineteenth century status became more important. Local dignitaries, members of parliament and office-holders in the denomination were sought; the names of Albert Spicer JP MP, a member of a prominent Congregational family in Essex, and David Williams Wire, the first nonconformist Lord Mayor of London, appeared on

An important person would draw a large crowd to watch the laying of a foundation stone, ensuring a report in the local press - and the collection of a large sum of money towards the building fund.

foundation stones across the county. More recently the names of the architect and builder were included.

Baptist chapels have, usually, more stones than other denominations; Pier Avenue, Clacton-on-Sea, has eleven, South Benfleet thirty-three while West Ham Central Mission is encircled by some 150, most representing congregations throughout the country. Small Methodists chapels, specially in the north-east of the county, have a stone over the door inscribed with the title and date, as at Thorpe-le-Soken, 'Primitive Methodist Chapel 1867'.

Of the many in the county, two have been chosen for special mention, both from Baptist chapels. One, at West Ham, celebrates the mile of half crowns collected by the Women's League towards the cost of the building. The other was laid by Master Bernard Farrow on behalf of the Sunday School and CE Society at Chingford Mount's first chapel in 1938; it was customary for the Superintendent to represent the Sunday School, and unusual at that time for a child to be given this honour.

Small date plaques over the door are found in the north-east of the county. The word 'Primitive' was erased from Little Bromley chapel after Methodist Union in the 1930s.

The foundation stone at West Ham Central Mission commemorating the work of the women in collecting a mile of half crowns towards the cost of the building.

Some of the 150 foundation stones encircling West Ham Central Mission.

ARCHITECTS

James Fenton's design for the new Congregational chapel at Braintree, 1832.
Reproduced by courtesy of Essex Record Office.

Early Meeting Houses were built in the vernacular but by the middle of the nineteenth century architects were being employed to design chapels. Jobson, writing in 1850, warned against the dangers of economising by accepting the offer of a design from a non-professional as experience had shown that problems could emerge later which were difficult to rectify. He urged Wesleyans to employ an architect who was at least sympathetic to Methodist expression in building, if not Methodist himself, with proven experience in chapel building.[20] The profession of Architect had been formalised in England in 1834 with the founding of the RIBA to establish standards of qualification.

In the Baptist Handbooks and Congregational Year Books a large number of architects employed by congregations throughout the country are noted, most contributing two or three buildings each. Within Essex four architects, in addition to the two already mentioned, have each made a particular contribution:

First, James Fenton (c1805 - 1875), a Congregationalist, who worked in Chelmsford for part of his career and is best known for his development of the New London Road area. He designed the Congregational chapels at

Billericay, Braintree, Ingatestone and Wivenhoe and the nonconformist cemetery at Chelmsford. He also designed the Strict Baptist chapel at Chelmsford in part exchange for their earlier site in Duke Street. Although Wivenhoe and Braintree were classical, he employed an austere Early English style for the other three, probably the first architect to do so within the county.[21]

The obituary of George Baines of London (1852 - 1934) noted that he had, together with his son, nearly 200 chapels to his name.[22] At least seventeen of these were in Essex, most

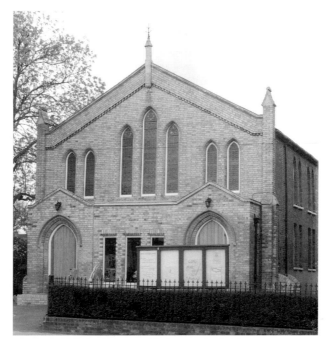

James Fenton was probably the first to change from classical style to Early English in his designs for chapels in Essex. Ingatestone Congregational chapel, 1840.

Crowstone Congregational chapel, Southend, designed by George Baines in 1924, shortly before he retired.

within the metropolitan area of the county. He began work at a time when nonconformists were building almost exclusively in the Gothic and most of his work continued in the same style; shortly before his retirement he added the new Gothic chapel to Crowstone Congregational, Southend. Pevsner, no admirer of nonconformist architecture, described his Methodist chapel in Katherine Road, East Ham, as 'pretty fancy Neo-Perp of that date...'.[23]

A very different contribution was made by William Hayne of Frinton and London. He worked in the first decades of the twentieth century at a time of greater freedom and experiment. He drew on the Byzantine style for his inspiration for West Ham Central Mission and Pier Avenue Baptist, Clacton-on-Sea, while choosing Art Nouveau decoration for Victoria Road South Baptist, Chelmsford and Frinton Free chapel. Different again is Hutton Mount Union chapel, with its deep tiled roof and dark

William Hayne followed the early twentieth century fashion for a chancel containing the organ, choir and communion table, together with transepts and a raked floor, but interpreted it in a light, spacious way at Hutton Mount Union chapel (1913).

timber bands, designed specially to harmonise with the wooded area within which it stands.

Post war, Kenneth Cheeseman has designed and remodelled more than twenty chapels in Essex, mostly Methodist.[24] He uses high windows and stained glass to create a light, spacious impression in his buildings. His Castle Methodist, Colchester, includes stained glass from the previous chapel and houses the pulpit from which Wesley preached in the town; the building won a civic award. Rayleigh Baptist incorporates the original chapel in an unusual enlargement, while Lighthouse Methodist, Walthamstow, has been remodelled inside to provide space for weekday activities on the ground floor while retaining much of the original furnishings, and atmosphere, in a smaller worship area upstairs.

Castle Methodist chapel, Colchester, designed by Kenneth Cheeseman in 1970, won a civic award.

PAYING FOR CHAPELS

It needs also to be emphasised that Dissent, unlike conformity, made considerable and continuous demands on the worshipper's purse...'.[25] Dissenters had to fund their own places of worship and support the minister, in addition to paying Church Rates (until 1868). Regular subscriptions were sought, and the pews were 'farmed', as Jobson termed the practice of letting sittings - hence the numbering of chapel pews.[26]

In the Independent Meeting House at Witham (1715) rents were fixed at five shillings to one guinea downstairs and half a crown to ten shillings upstairs. Subscribers had a choice of pew in order, according to the size of their contribution to funds; in cases of equal contribution, the order was decided by lot.[27] At Bocking Independent, the Trust Deed of 1708 stated that seats were to be given to heirs unless unused for six months. Seats which became vacant were to be given to those likely to contribute most to the maintenance. The poor were allowed to sit at the Table Pew.[28]

During the eighteenth and early nineteenth centuries ministers went on begging tours to raise money for building or repairing Meeting Houses. Congregations resented their ministers being away for long periods, specially when the results did not justify the efforts. London was seen as a fruitful area and subjected to many

A pew number at Weeley Wesleyan Methodist chapel, necessary when pews were rented out as a means of paying off the debt on the building.

requests. The situation was addressed by each denomination. In 1770 when debt had mounted Wesley banned all new building unless it could be paid for in full. From 1793 District Meetings could authorise new projects but debts continued to grow so a general Chapel Fund was formed in 1818 to help pay these off. Baptists had to apply to the Baptist Board or Case Committee in the eighteenth century, and the centralised London Baptist Building Fund was set up in 1824. The Congregational Union was founded in 1832, one of its functions being to assist chapel building without the nuisance of begging, but a reluctance to contribute made this aspect of its work ineffective. The London Congregational Building Fund was eventually set up in 1848.[29]

The burden of funding still lay with the individual chapel. Subscriptions were requested, and a loan would make up the difference; pew rents serviced the loan. Some members were able to contribute more, as for example at Upminster first Congregational three subscriptions made the major part of the cost. A few chapels were fortunate enough to receive gifts of land, as at Dunmow Strict Baptist and Clacton-on-Sea Wesleyan, while Wivenhoe third Congregational chapel was paid for entirely by Thomas Sandford, a ship owner and trader who lived nearby.

Differential rents perpetuated social divisions; a writer recalled his impressions of Rayleigh Particular Baptist chapel in the 1860s: 'It had the old square pews for the farmers and their families under the gallies, the benches upstairs for farmers' work people, and the central pews for shopkeepers and other denizens of the town.'[30]

The Religious Census of 1851 records the number of free and other sittings in each place of worship. In Tendring Hundred an average of one third of sittings in chapels were free, whereas Anglicans offered two thirds of their sittings without rent. Free sittings in chapel used to be of inferior quality, often benches which might not have a back.

Towards the end of the nineteenth century weekly collections were introduced and pew rents declined in importance. Social gatherings such as anniversaries, tea meetings, stone-laying and chapel openings were seen as opportunities to gather funds, the amount collected being reported in the press account of the occasion. The Baptist Handbooks in the nineteenth century recorded the cost of new chapels and the amount of debt reduced or paid off each year.

The Baptist Loan Fund and English Congregational Chapel-Building Fund continued into this century. The President of the London Baptist Union made one new chapel his special cause during his year of office and several Essex chapels benefited in this way, among them East Ham and Higham Hill.[31]

Today, with the closure of so many chapels, particularly in rural areas, the sale of redundant sites may contribute to the funding of new buildings within the denomination. However money is hard to find, so congregations look for alternative schemes where possible. The new Strict Baptist chapel at Walthamstow is contained within a block of flats, while two chapels already mentioned have incorporated shops into their buildings; each of these provides a continuing source of income. Others share a building with another congregation and sell one of their previous sites, as at Brightlingsea where the United Reformed congregation share the Methodist building, their own serving as business premises. Some have found themselves in an area which is to be redeveloped, and have taken the opportunity to redesign their buildings to meet present needs, for example the United Reformed congregations at Chelmsford and Romford.

INTO THE FUTURE

High Woods Methodist chapel, 1999, one of the most recent to be opened in an area of new housing.

Closure of chapels has become a familiar, though sad, occurrence, specially in rural areas. Some find a new lease of life in alternative use; small buildings convert readily to homes while in towns they make storage or office space. Some continue in religious use by one of the smaller sects, or - in three cases - by Roman Catholics. In Newham, chapel buildings serve the local community as work-shops, advice or resource centres or multi-faith places of worship.

But that is not the whole picture. With new housing come new chapels, as at North Springfield Baptist, Chelmsford, or Highwoods Methodist, Colchester. Congregations are finding a variety of ways of sharing buildings, either keeping their separate denominational identity or forming a single congregation; Leytonstone has a Union chapel (Baptist and URC) while Methodists and URC share build-ings at Braintree, Brightlingsea and Walton-on-the-Naze. Unthinkable a century ago, some now join with the established church, as at Christchurch URC & Anglican, Colchester, while at Beckton and South Woodham Ferrers a single building serves nonconformist, Anglican and Roman Catholic needs.

Interest in chapels is being fostered by the Chapels Society which also offers advice where change is being considered. The recent growth of studies in Family and Local History also brings chapels to notice. Books about Church architecture are beginning to include chapels and the Royal Commission on the Historical Monuments of England's Inventory of historic Nonconformist Chapels and Meeting-houses is almost complete. Redundant chapels of architectural importance are being restored and made accessible to the public by the Historic Chapels Trust. This ground swell of interest should ensure that chapels receive the attention they deserve and find their rightful place within our culture.

New towns, developed as congregations were diminishing, have seen the greatest advances in shared accommodation. A single building serves the needs of nonconformists, Anglicans and Roman Catholics at Staple Tye, Harlow (left), and South Woodham Ferrers (below).

ADDRESSES

THE CHAPELS SOCIETY Correspondent: Mrs C. van Melzen,
Rookery Farmhouse, Laxfield, Suffolk IP13 8JA.

The Society seeks to promote public interest and knowledge of the architectural and historical importance of nonconformist places of worship. It also seeks to promote the survival of chapel buildings and furnishings by offering advice and encouragement to those responsible for their upkeep. It works closely with the Historic Chapels Trust.

HISTORIC CHAPELS TRUST   29 Thurloe Street, London SW7 2LQ.

The Trust takes into ownership redundant chapels of outstanding architectural and historic interest in order to secure for public benefit their presentation, repair and maintenance.

REFERENCES

1   J. Stevens, *The Victorian Church* (1995) and C. Brooks, A. Saint, *The Victorian Church: Architecture and Society* (1995) each contain a chapter on nonconformist architecture.

2   M.R. Watts, *The Dissenters Vol I* (1978), 509.

3   *Ibid*, 277.

4   A.G. Matthews, *Calamy Revised* (1934).

5   *Ibid*.

6   M.R. Watts, *op.cit.*, 303.

7   R.W. Dixon, 'Reminiscences of the Old Dissent at Witham', *TCHS*, 5 (1911-12), 336-337.

8   W.H. Beckett, *Sketches of Free Church Life at Stebbing, Essex* (1893).

9   The Evans List, Dr. Williams Library. Ms 38.4.

10 N. Curnock (Ed), *The Journal of Rev J. Wesley* (1909-16).

11 D.W. Dolby, *The Architectural Expression of Methodism* (1964).

12 F. Tillyard, 'The Distribution of the Free Churches in England', *Sociological Review*, XXVI (1938), 1-18; see also M.R. Watts, *The Dissenters Vol II* (1995), 35-48.

13 *Congregational Year Book* (1847), 150.

14 W.Y. Fullerton, *C.H. Spurgeon, a biography* (1920), 137.

15 *Congregational Year Book* (1847), 161.

16 *Ibid*, 162.

17 F.J. Jobson, *Chapel and School Architecture* (1850).

18 Essex Record Office, D/N 52/5/2.

19 M.J. Turner, *Mill Hill to Overshot Bridge*.

20 F.J. Jobson, *op.cit.*, 166.

21 H. Colvin, *A Biographical Dictionary of British Architects* 1600-1840 (1978).

22 *The Builder*, 23 March 1934, 494.

23 N. Pevsner, *The Buildings of England, Essex* (1965), 166.

24 Personal communication.

25 M.R. Watts, *Vol I op.cit.*, 358.

26 F.J. Jobson, *op.cit.*, 66.

27 M.L. Smith, *A Brief History of Witham Congregational Church* (1965).

28 Essex Record Office, D/NC 52/5/2.

29 M.R. Watts, *Vol II op.cit.* 222-240.

30 Essex Record Office, D/NB 2/2.

31 W.C. Johnson, *Encounters in London* (1965), Appendix B.

DIRECTORY

Section One contains buildings which still exist, whatever their present use, while Section Two lists buildings which have been demolished and not replaced. The parts of Essex which now constitute London Boroughs are listed separately from the rest of Essex. The information was gathered in 1996-98, with minor later additions.

The date of the foundation stone of a building is given where possible in preference to that of the formation of the congregation or opening of the chapel. The sequence of dates of buildings belonging to a congregation is given, although some earlier chapels may have been on a different site. Where a congregation closed its building and moved to join with another congregation, this is indicated by letters in square brackets, for example Braintree Methodist congregation [a] sold its building and joined with the United Reformed congregation [A].

The list, specially in Section Two, cannot be precise in every detail, despite every effort to make it so. A reference to a congregation does not necessarily imply the existence of a chapel, while some 'shadowy causes' known to have existed at certain dates have no known beginning or end. The writer would be pleased to receive additions and amendments.

* An asterisk indicates that the chapel is featured in the illustrations.

SECTION ONE: Buildings which still stand.

A) Present-day Essex.
B) London Boroughs which used to be part of Essex.

The information is given in the following order:
1   Place.
2   Denomination of the founding congregation; if this changed within a few years of building the second is also given.
3   Dates of past and present buildings of the congregation.
4   Present use of the building: the denomination, or 'religious' (a denomination or faith other than those included in the study), or secular, or empty.
5   Map reference of present building.
6   Additional information.

SECTION TWO: Chapels which have been demolished and not replaced.

A) Present-day Essex.
B) London Boroughs which used to be part of Essex.

The information is given in the following order:
1   Place.
2   Denomination of the founding congregation; if the denomination changed within a few years both are given.
3   Dates of buildings (or first available date).
4   Date of closure or demolition (or last available date).
5   Map reference of the latest chapel.
6   Additional information.

SECTION ONE A

Buildings which still stand in present-day Essex.

ABRIDGE
Wesleyan Methodist/
Congregational, 1833, secular,
TQ477946.

ALTHORNE
Primitive Methodist, 1856,
secular, TQ907999. Now a house.

ARDLEIGH
Primitive Methodist, 1859, empty,
TM039262.
Wesleyan Methodist, 1821,
Methodist, TM052294. Altered
and extended later.

ARKESDEN
Wesleyan Methodist, 1887,
secular, TL478346. Now a house.

ASHDON
Particular Baptist, 1833, Baptist,
TL588420. Box pews; baptistry in
the pulpit.

AVELEY
Independent, 1817, 1877, United
Reformed, TQ565802. By Sulman.
Methodist, 1960, Methodist,
TQ562809. By George Baines and
Syborn.

BADDOW, GREAT
Independent, 1848, 1986, United
Reformed, TL728050. The two
buildings were amalgamated to
form the present chapel, by Marsh
Eddison Brown.
Peculiar People, 1880, religious,
TL729049.

BADDOW, LITTLE
*Presbyterian/Independent, 1707,
United Reformed, TL766077.
Two oval windows on the long
wall indicate where the pulpit
used to be.

BARDFIELD, GREAT
Primitive Methodist, 1862,
secular, TL675306. Now a house.
Society of Friends, by 1708
(adopted), 1806, Society of
Friends, TL676305.

BARLING
Peculiar People, 1926, religious,
TQ930891.

BASILDON
Baptist, 1931, Baptist, TQ679876.
*Strict Baptist, 1953, Baptist
(Grace), TQ723898. The first
purpose-built chapel in the New
Town; by E.J. Wood.
Baptist, 1958, Baptist, TQ707878.
Front extension in 1994.
Congregational, 1959, United
Reformed, TQ708891.
Wesleyan Methodist, 1907, 1956,
Methodist, TQ679878.
Wesleyan Methodist, 1929, 1980,
Methodist, TQ738856. The
earlier building is now a hall.
Methodist, 1959, Methodist,
TQ723880. Preceded by Gordon
Hall.
Methodist, 1967, Methodist,
TQ693889.

BATTLESBRIDGE
Congregational, 1844,
Congregational, TQ780947.

BEAUMONT-CUM-MOZE
Wesleyan Methodist, 1825,1877,
Methodist, TM168250.

BENFLEET, SOUTH
Baptist, 1923, Baptist, TQ775870.
Encircled by thirty three
foundation stones and twenty one
initialled bricks.
Wesleyan Methodist, 1877, 1931,
Methodist, TQ777863.

BENTLEY, GREAT
Wesleyan Methodist, 1819, 1843,
Methodist, TM111219. The
worship area has been reduced
and redesigned.
Wesleyan Methodist, 1889,
secular, TM117204. Now a house.

BENTLEY, LITTLE
Wesleyan Methodist, 1811, 1870,
empty, TM118256.

BERDEN
Wesleyan Methodist, c1860,
1907, secular, TL469298. Now
the Village Hall.

BERGHOLT, WEST
Primitive Methodist, 1838, 1879,
Methodist, TL961275.

BILLERICAY
Baptist, c1800, 1812, 1829,
c1882, 1964, Baptist, TQ674957.
*Presbyterian/Independent, 1714,
1838, United Reformed, TQ675943.
Early English by J. Fenton.
Congregational, 1928, religious,
TQ683946. By Ford Duncanson.
Wesleyan Methodist, 1925, 1963,
Methodist, TQ671947.
Society of Friends, by 1698
(closed by 1800), 1958 (adopted),
Society of Friends, TQ675940.

BLACKMORE
Particular Baptist, 1843, Baptist,
TL604018.

BOWERS GIFFORD
Congregational, 1885, religious,
TQ748882.

BOXTED
Wesleyan Methodist, 1831,
Methodist, TM003313.

BRADFIELD
*Wesleyan Methodist, c1789,
1850, Methodist, TM140300.

BRADWELL
Congregational, 1932,
Congregational, TL806229.

BRAINTREE
Particular Baptist, 1760, 1833,
Baptist, TL758231. Classical.
*Independent, 1707,
Congregational, TL757234.
Altered in 1818.
*Independent, 1788, 1832,
Methodist & United Reformed,
TL754227. Classical, by J.
Fenton. [A]
Congregational, 1862, United
Reformed, TL761260.
Congregational, 1933,
Congregational, TL771233.
Primitive Methodist, 1862,
religious, TL761230.

BRENTWOOD
Particular Baptist, 1885, 1915,
Baptist, TQ592933.
Presbyterian/Congregational, by
1717, c1753, 1847, United
Reformed, TQ594936. Classical.

BRENTWOOD continued
Congregational, 1868, 1906,
Baptist & Congregational,
TQ624946.

*Union (Baptist &
Congregational), 1913, Union,
TQ613944. By W. Hayne.
Wesleyan Methodist, 1842, 1878,
1892, Methodist, TQ593929.
Refronted in 1970. The second
building continues in religious use.
Peculiar People, 1863, secular,
TQ628912.
Society of Friends, 1957, Society
of Friends, TQ609948. By H.M.
Lidbetter.

BRIGHTLINGSEA
Independent, 1833, 1865, secular,
TM090170. Used by a business;
by H. Darken. [b]

*Wesleyan Methodist, 1805, 1843,
Methodist & United Reformed,
TM092169. The interior is largely
unaltered. [B]

BROMLEY, GREAT
Primitive Methodist, 1861, empty,
TM067276.

*Wesleyan Methodist, 1837,
empty, TM093242.

BROMLEY, LITTLE
*Primitive Methodist, 1863, empty,
TM099289.

BROOMFIELD
*Primitive Methodist, 1910, 1963,
Methodist, TL708096. By C. and
W. Pertwee.

BROXTED
Congregational, 1852,
Congregational, TL565249.

BUCKHURST HILL
Particular Baptist, 1866, secular,
TQ410939. Became a library. A
subsequent iron building has been
demolished.
Congregational, 1863, c1925,
secular, TQ418938.

*Congregational, 1866, 1874,
1955, United Reformed,
TQ409940. The tower of the
1874 Gothic chapel, by E. Egan,
still stands.
Congregational/Baptist, 1909
(adopted), 1966, Baptist,
TQ413939.

BULMER
Congregational, 1875, secular,
TL840401. Now a house.

BURNHAM-ON-CROUCH
General Baptist/Particular Baptist,
by 1715, 1833, 1904, Baptist,
TQ950957.
Presbyterian/Independent, 1862,
1950, United Reformed,
TQ949961.
Primitive Methodist, 1865,
secular, TQ950959. The polychrome brickwork earned it the
name 'six of diamonds'.

CANEWDON
Congregational, 1833, c1983,
Congregational, TQ899945.

CANVEY ISLAND
Baptist, 1920, Baptist, TQ809833.
Baptist, 1926, 1982, Baptist,
TQ791844.
Methodist, 1959, Methodist,
TQ797837.

CHAPPEL
Congregational, 1901, United
Reformed, TL900282.

CHELMSFORD
Strict and Particular Baptist,
1803, 1848, Strict and Particular
Baptist (Grace), TL707064. Early
English by J. Fenton.

*Baptist, 1908, Baptist, TL705069.
Art Nouveau decoration, by W.
Hayne.
Baptist, 1935, Baptist, TL723069.

*Baptist, 1982, Baptist, TL725084.
A striking modern design with a
long sloping roof.
Congregational, 1928, United
Reformed, TL699080.
Congregational, 1955, United
Reformed, TL684082.
Congregational, 1970, United
Reformed, TL703061. By J.
Finch; a large complex with
rooms below the worship area. [C]
Primitive Methodist, 1863,
Methodist, TL709062. By T.
Moss (elder).
Wesleyan Methodist, 1813, 1843,
1898, 1961, TL702072. By
Cubitt-Nichols.
Methodist, 1961, Methodist,
TL709047.

Peculiar People, c1900, 1931,
religious, TL708061.

*Society of Friends, by 1667, 1701,
1790, 1824, 1958, Society of
Friends, TL701073. The 1824
Meeting House by J. Collis, a
classical building with pillared
portico and pediment, is now used
by Anglia University. The present
building by P.V. Mauger.

CHESTERFORD, GREAT
Independent/Union, 1841,
Congregational, TL508429.
Unusual decorative brickwork.

CHIGNAL ST JAMES
Baptist, 1926, Baptist, TL684089.
An iron chapel.

CHIGNAL SMEALEY
Congregational, 1842, United
Reformed, TL660118.

CHIGWELL ROW
*Congregational, 1804, United
Reformed, TQ459931.

CHIPPING ONGAR
Presbyterian/Independent, 1720,
1833, United Reformed,
TL552028. Classical by J. Sadd.

CHRISHALL
Primitive Methodist, 1871,
Methodist, TL445398.

CLACTON-ON-SEA
*Baptist, 1902, 1908, 1928, Baptist,
TM172149. The second, iron,
building is used as a Hall. The
1928 building by W. Hayne in the
Byzantine style.

*Union (Baptist & Congregational),
1886, United Reformed, TM178148.
Gothic with transepts and tower.
By T.H. Baker.
Primitive Methodist, 1863, 1902,
religious, TM171151.
Wesleyan Methodist, 1877,
Methodist, TM173148. Gothic
with spire.
Wesleyan Methodist, 1893,
Methodist, TM160154.
Methodist, 1966, Methodist,
TM153138.
Society of Friends, 1947 (adopted),
Society of Friends, TM178152.

CLACTON, GREAT
Wesleyan Methodist, 1824, 1876,
Methodist, TM177163.

CLACTON, LITTLE
  Wesleyan Methodist, 1851,
  Methodist, TM164191.
  Y-mullioned windows.
CLAVERING
  Independent, 1692, c1800, 1872,
  United Reformed, TL473317,
  Triple windows flanking the
  double doors. By Sulman and
  Rhodes.
  *Primitive Methodist, 1844, 1877,
  Methodist, TL481323.
COGGESHALL
  Particular Baptist, 1780, 1829,
  1855, secular, TL850227. Pilasters
  and pediment in brick. [d]
  *Independent, 1710, Baptist &
  Methodist & United Reformed,
  TL849227. Enlarged and altered
  several times. Plaque to John
  Owen in the porch. [D]
  Wesleyan Methodist, 1847, 1882,
  TL849226. Now a Hall for the
  shared chapel.[d]
  Society of Friends, by 1670, early
  1700s, 1878, secular, TL849227.
  Now a Library.
COLCHESTER
  Particular Baptist, 1690, 1711,
  1834, Baptist, TL997250.
  Classical; the baptistry is now to
  the left of the pulpit.
  Particular Baptist, 1885, Baptist,
  TM022265.
  Baptist, 1905, 1992, Baptist,
  TM003219. The first building
  continues as a Hall.
  Strict and Particular Baptist,
  1812, 1872, 1964, Baptist
  (Grace), TL972240.
  *Independent, 1691, 1735, 1766,
  1863, 1986, United Reformed,
  TL997250. Octagonal (as was the
  1766 building) with shops on the
  ground floor, by D. Roberts. The
  spire of the 1863 Gothic building
  by F. Barnes still stands.
  *Congregational, 1816, secular,
  TL996254. Classical facade added
  in 1836.
  Congregational, 1842, 1954, 1993,
  United Reformed, TL972236. The
  first chapel continues in religious
  use.

  *Congregational, 1844, 1977,
  United Reformed & Anglican,
  TL985244. The earlier classical
  building by Poulton continues in
  secular use.
  Congregational, 1844, 1938,
  United Reformed, TM011253.
  *Congregational, 1869,
  Congregational, TM016229. An
  iron chapel.
  Congregational, 1935,
  Congregational, TL961248.
  Primitive Methodist, 1839,
  religious, TM008246.
  Primitive Methodist, 1859,
  Methodist, TL963249
  Primitive Methodist, 1873,
  secular, TL995254.
  *Wesleyan Methodist, 1759, 1800,
  1835, 1928, 1970, Methodist,
  TL997252. By K. Cheeseman;
  includes stained glass from the
  1928 chapel and the pulpit from
  which Wesley preached.
  Wesleyan Methodist, 1895,
  Methodist, TL988280.
  Wesleyan Methodist, 1904,
  Methodist, TM006243. Free
  Gothic with tower and matching
  Hall.
  *Methodist, 1999, Methodist,
  TM010282.
  Peculiar People, 1866, 1991,
  religious, TL954247.
  Society of Friends, 1663,1683
  (adopted), 1801, 1872, 1938,
  1971 (adopted), Society of Friends,
  TL993251. The second building,
  the ancient St Helen's chapel, was
  used by Friends for over a century,
  and still stands. The present
  building was converted from a
  Georgian house; the added
  Meeting Room is hexagonal.
COLNE, EARLS
  Particular Baptist, 1786, 1818, 1860,
  Baptist, TL853289.
  *Society of Friends, 1674, possibly
  1733, Society of Friends, TL856290.
  Pyramid roof with pantiles.
COLNE, WHITE
  Particular Baptist, 1843, secular,
  TL870289. Now a house.

COPFORD
  Society of Friends, 1727, 1879,
  1923, secular, TL930240. Now a
  house.
CORRINGHAM
  Baptist, 1938, Baptist, TQ700836.
  *Peculiar People, 1914, religious,
  TQ711838.
CRESSING
  Peculiar People, 1909, religious,
  TL792208.
DANBURY
  *Congregational, 1937, United
  Reformed, TL785053. By F.
  Lawrence.
DEBDEN
  Congregational, 1858, secular,
  TL557334. Now a house.
DEDHAM
  Independent, 1738, 1871, secular,
  TM058331. By Sulman and
  Rhodes; now an Arts Centre.
  Primitive Methodist, 1863,
  Methodist, TM067314.
DOVERCOURT
  Primitive Methodist, 1866,
  Methodist, TM236310.
  Wesleyan Methodist, 1905,
  Methodist & United Reformed,
  TM253314. Gothic facade. [E]
DUNMOW
  Strict and Particular Baptist,
  1880, Strict Baptist (Grace),
  TL627218.
  *Independent, by 1715, 1869,
  United Reformed, TL628216. By
  C. Pertwee in Romanesque style.
  *Society of Friends, 1706, 1833,
  Society of Friends, TL627216.
EASTER, GOOD
  Congregational, 1853, secular,
  TL629125. Now a house.
EASTER, HIGH
  Independent, 1822, 1847, secular,
  TL621147. Now a house.
EIGHT ASH GREEN
  Primitive Methodist, 1866, 1934,
  Methodist, TL942257.
ELMSTEAD
  *Wesleyan Methodist, 1817, 1863,
  Methodist, TM065245.

EPPING

Presbyterian/Independent, 1693, 1774, 1997, United Reformed, TL462027. The chapel was demolished in 1997 while the Hall was refurbished to be used for worship.

Wesleyan Methodist, 1878, 1887, Methodist, TL458020. Gothic.

Society of Friends, 1705, 1850, Society of Friends, TL463023. By W. Beck.

EPPING GREEN

Union, 1834, 1862, religious, TL435055. The first chapel continues as a house.

FELSTED

Independent, 1833, 1923, United Reformed, TL678204. The Gothic chapel is now in secular use, while the later Hall is used for services.

FINCHINGFIELD

Presbyterian/Independent, c1700, 1779, United Reformed, TL683328. Pediment and portico; two galleries now hidden by false ceiling.

FINGRINGHOE

Primitive Methodist, 1847, 1874, 1934, Methodist, TM025198.

FORDHAM

Congregational (Countess of Huntingdon), 1790, secular, TL931293. Pyramid roof; now a house.

FOXEARTH

Independent, 1787, secular, TL834445. Hipped roof with pantiles.

FRINTON-ON-SEA

*Baptist, 1911, Baptist, TM237194. By W. Hayne; curved pews and raked floor.

Wesleyan Methodist, 1903, Methodist, TM234199. Gothic facade.

GALLEYWOOD

Primitive Methodist, 1860, Methodist, TL708027.

GOLDHANGER

Wesleyan Methodist, 1839, secular, TL903087.

GOSFIELD

Primitive Methodist, c1900, secular, TL778272. An iron building, now a house.

GRAYS

Particular Baptist, 1885, 1893, Baptist, TQ616782. By C. Cobham.

Baptist, 1898, 1933, Baptist, TQ624793. The earlier building continues in religious use.

Baptist, 1915, secular, TQ598778.

Baptist, 1957, Baptist, TQ614803.

Congregational, 1858, 1886, 1956, United Reformed, TQ619789. A stained glass window from the second, Gothic, building by E.C. Allam is incorporated in the present building.

Methodist, 1939, Methodist, TQ617793.

Methodist, 1959, Methodist, TQ643784.

Peculiar People, 1892, Baptist (Grace), TQ620779.

Peculiar People, 1901, secular TQ618779.

HADLEIGH

Baptist, 1926, Baptist, TQ806875.

Congregational, 1904, United Reformed, TQ811871. Later extensions.

*Wesleyan Methodist, 1865, 1929, Methodist, TQ805871.

Peculiar People, 1853, 1880, 1976, religious, TQ812886. A wooden building.

Peculiar People, 1893, secular, TQ807888. Now a house.

HADSTOCK

Independent, by 1863, secular, TL560448. Now a house.

HALLINGBURY, LITTLE

(Mission), 1877, Congregational, TL498169.

HALSTEAD

Particular Baptist, 1799, 1816, 1967, Baptist, TL814307.

Strict and Particular Baptist, 1836, 1876, 1909, Baptist (Grace), TL817305.

Baptist, 1960, Baptist, TL808296.

*Independent, 1679, 1718, 1865, empty, TL815305. Decorated Gothic with transepts; school-rooms underneath. By F. Barnes.

Primitive Methodist, 1874, Methodist, TL809303.

Society of Friends, by 1664, 1851, secular, TL816307.

HARLOW

*Strict Baptist, 1756, Baptist, TL472086. Georgian facade with a fine door; interior modernised.

Particular Baptist, 1764, 1865, Baptist, TL470114. Italianate.

Congregational, 1958, United Reformed, TL453102.

Wesleyan Methodist, 1886, Methodist, TL476116.

Methodist, 1954, Methodist, TL458106.

Methodist & Anglican & Roman Catholic, 1968, Methodist & Anglican & Roman Catholic, TL443081. Polygonal with raised roof light.

Presbyterian (CoE), 1955, United Reformed, TL439096.

Society of Friends, 1962, Society of Friends, TL456090. By N. Frith.

HARWICH

*Wesleyan Methodist/Strict Baptist, 1821, secular, TM260327. Now a workshop.

HATFIELD BROAD OAK

Congregational, 1868, religious, TL548165.

HATFIELD HEATH

*Presbyterian/Independent, by 1715, 1725, 1875, United Reformed, TL526149. Gothic, by T. Lewis Banks. An asymmetric stained glass window, and large clock behind the pulpit.

HATFIELD PEVEREL

Wesleyan Methodist, 1826, 1874, Methodist, TL788117. Gothic with a spire.

HAWKWELL

Baptist, 1927, Baptist, TQ863919.

HEDINGHAM, CASTLE

*Presbyterian/Independent, 1719, 1842, United Reformed, TL784353. Pediment and pilasters.

HEDINGHAM, SIBLE

Particular Baptist, 1807, Baptist, TL779344. Square with hipped roof.

Strict Baptist, 1864, Strict Baptist, TL783340. Polychrome brickwork.

Society of Friends/Congregational,
1675, 1813, 1874, secular,
TL782338.

HEMPSTEAD
Primitive Methodist, 1853,
secular, TL633379. Now a house.

HENHAM
Congregational, 1864, secular,
TL545284. Now a house.

HEYBRIDGE
Congregational, 1900,
Congregational, TL862090.

HIGH GARRET
Unitarian, 1853, (1895), secular,
TL776269. (The later building in
Braintree has been demolished.)

HOCKLEY
Congregational, 1929, United
Reformed, TQ839925.
Wesleyan Methodist, 1883
(adopted), 1906, Methodist,
TQ836924. Gothic.
Peculiar People, 1922, religious,
TQ844929.

HOLLAND-ON-SEA
Baptist, 1956, Baptist, TM200167.
Wesleyan Methodist, 1925, 1969,
Methodist, TM194162. The
window in the extended roof
lights the communion table. The
earlier building is now used as a
Hall.

HOLLAND, GREAT
Wesleyan Methodist, 1891, 1927,
Methodist, TM213194. A spire.
The earlier building is now a
house.

HORKESLEY, GREAT
Baptist/Independent, by 1837,
religious, TL979295. A square
chapel with extension.
Primitive Methodist, 1862,
secular, TL977306. Now the
Village Hall.

HORNDON-ON-THE-HILL
*Wesleyan Methodist, 1885, 1890,
Methodist, TQ670834.

HULLBRIDGE
Congregational, 1938,
Congregational, TQ808940.

INGATESTONE
*Independent, 1813, 1840, United
Reformed, TQ648994. Early
English by J.Fenton.

KELVEDON
Independent, 1814, 1853, United
Reformed, TL860188. Pediment
and Pilasters in brick.
Society of Friends, 1802, empty,
TL864192.

KELVEDON HATCH
Wesleyan Methodist, 1879,
secular, TQ568990.

KIRBY
Baptist, 1943, Baptist,
TM222208. Converted from a
bungalow.
Primitive Methodist, 1855, 1874,
Methodist, TM214209. The
earlier chapel is still in use as a
Hall.
Primitive Methodist, 1889, 1926,
religious, TM222220.

LANGHAM
Primitive Methodist, 1837, 1960,
secular, TM016315. Now a house.

LANGLEY
Particular Baptist, 1828, 1892,
Baptist (Grace), TL445350. By
Buchere Abrams.
*Primitive Methodist, 1862,
Methodist, TL437342.

LATCHINGDON
Congregational, 1908, religious,
TL882004.

LAVER, HIGH
Congregational/Methodist, 1877,
secular, TL497096. Now a house.

LAYER BRETON
Independent, c1790, 1860,
secular, TL945188. Now a garage.

LAYER-DE-LA-HAYE
Congregational, 1843, secular,
TL965200.

LEIGHS, GREAT
Baptist, 1934, Baptist, TL730176.

LOUGHTON
Baptist, 1813, 1860, 1972,
Baptist, TQ419959. The second
chapel was Italianate.
Congregational, 1953, United
Reformed, TQ435963.
Wesleyan Methodist, 1873
(adopted), 1881, 1903, 1986,
Methodist, TQ423965. By B.
Gooding; uses Swedish timber

portal frames in its construction.
Methodist & Anglican, 1962,
Methodist & Anglican,
TQ441972.

MALDON
Particular Baptist, 1872, 1887,
1896, Baptist, TL852070.
*Independent, by 1715, 1801,
United Reformed, TL851071.
Refronted with pediment and
pillared portico. An oval gallery
encircles the chapel.
Primitive Methodist, 1861,
religious, TL852068.
Wesleyan Methodist, 1824, 1861,
Methodist, TL854069. The earlier
building continues in secular use
as a Labour Hall.
Society of Friends, 1707, 1821,
Society of Friends, TL853070.

MANNINGTREE
Congregational, 1823, secular,
TM106317. A 'square' chapel
with curved sash windows.
Wesleyan Methodist, 1795, 1807,
Methodist, TM107316. Classical
with almost unchanged interior.

MANUDEN
Primitive Methodist, 1880,
secular, TL486270. Now a house.

MARKS TEY
Wesleyan Methodist, 1903,
Methodist, TL921237.

MATCHING TYE
Congregational, 1876, secular,
TL516112. Now a house.

MERSEA, WEST
*Congregational, 1805, 1841,
Baptist & Congregational,
TM015133. A 'square' building
with added porch.
Wesleyan Methodist, 1848, 1861,
Methodist, TM014132.

MISTLEY
Primitive Methodist, 1862,
Methodist, TM121316.

MORETON
Congregational, 1862, secular,
TL531077.

MOUNT BURES
Strict and Particular Baptist,
1839, Strict Baptist, TL901311.

NAZEING
Congregational (Countess of
Huntingdon), 1816, 1876,
Congregational, TL400056.
Gothic.

NORTH WEALD BASSETT
Wesleyan Methodist, 1890, 1931,
Methodist, TL497040.

NOTLEY, BLACK
Congregational, 1893, 1991,
Baptist, TL770204. The first
building is still in use as a Room.

OAKLEY, GREAT
Wesleyan Methodist, 1824,
Methodist, TM193276. Unusual
doorways.

OAKLEY, LITTLE
*Wesleyan Methodist, c1800,
1863, 1969, Methodist,
TM219292.

OCKENDON, SOUTH
Independent, 1812, 1965, United
Reformed, TQ589815. The earlier,
'square', building stands empty.
Wesleyan Methodist, 1847,
Methodist, TQ592829.

ORSETT
*Congregational, 1843,
Congregational, TQ646817.
Early English.

PAGLESHAM
Congregational, 1856, 1962,
Congregational, TQ926924.

PANFIELD
Primitive Methodist, 1890,
secular, TL730254.

PARKESTON
Wesleyan Methodist, 1887,
Methodist, TM236321.

PEBMARSH
Particular Baptist, 1869
(adopted), secular, TL848336.
Now a house.

PURFLEET
Baptist, 1897, 1938, Baptist,
TQ562779. By A.G. Gentry.

PURLEIGH
Congregational, 1821, secular,
TL837016. Now a house.
Primitive Methodist, 1929, empty,
TL814029.

RADWINTER
Particular Baptist, 1852, empty,
TL612376.

RAMSDEN BELLHOUSE
Baptist, 1927, Baptist, TL719946.

RAMSDEN HEATH
Congregational, 1873, 1935,
Congregational, TQ711958. The
earlier building is now the Hall.

RAMSEY
Wesleyan Methodist, 1822, 1854,
Methodist, TM210304.
Y-mullioned windows.

RAYLEIGH
Particular Baptist, 1799, 1864,
1981, Baptist, TQ804907. The
first building is incorporated in
the recent redevelopment by K.
Cheeseman while the second
building serves as a Hall.
Baptist/Congregational, 1898,
United Reformed, TQ804907.
Gothic.
*Wesleyan Methodist, 1885, 1934,
Methodist, TQ809902. The earlier
building is still in religious use.
Peculiar People, c1900, 1923,
religious, TQ806904.

RAYNE
Congregational, 1907, secular,
TL721225. Now a house.

RETTENDON
Congregational, 1884, religious,
TQ755979.

RIDGEWELL
Presbyterian/Independent, by
1715, 1858, Congregational,
TL735411. Gothic.

RIVENHALL
Congregational, 1894, secular,
TL840165. Now a house.

ROCHFORD
Presbyterian/Independent, by
1715, 1741, Congregational,
TQ867906.
Wesleyan Methodist, 1822, 1841,
1880, Methodist, TQ875907.

RODING, WHITE
Congregational, 1886, secular,
TL564132. Now a house.

ROWHEDGE
Primitive Methodist, 1913, empty,
TM030217.

ROXWELL
Congregational, 1865,
Congregational, TL638062.

ROYDON
*Particular Baptist/Independent,
1798, 1851, United Reformed,
TL412100.

SAFFRON WALDEN
*General Baptist, 1729, 1792,
secular, TL539383. Double
hipped roof.
Particular Baptist, 1774, 1879,
Baptist, TL538381. Italianate.
Strict and Particular Baptist,
1822, secular, TL536380. Now a
house.
*Independent, 1694, 1811, United
Reformed, TL536383. Portico
and broken pediment.
Primitive Methodist, 1868,
secular, TL539386. Now a shop.
Wesleyan Methodist, 1824,
1865, Methodist, TL537387.
Society of Friends, 1676, 1791,
1879, Society of Friends,
TL537382.

ST OSYTH
*Wesleyan Methodist, 1834, 1855,
Methodist, TM124155.

SAMPFORD, GREAT
Particular Baptist, 1802, 1875,
Baptist, TL642353.

SANDON
Congregational, 1873, United
Reformed, TL747032.

SHALFORD
Congregational, 1854, 1954,
Congregational, TL712271.

SILVER END
Congregational, 1930,
Congregational, TL805198.

SOUTHEND
Eastwood
Baptist, 1911, 1970, Baptist,
TQ840890.
Congregational, 1939, United
Reformed, TQ830892.
Peculiar People, 1927, religious,
TQ837887.

Leigh-on-Sea
Baptist, 1893, 1908, 1927,
Baptist, TQ847860. Gothic with
tower.
Baptist, 1913, 1961, Baptist,
TQ839865. The earlier building
now serves as a Hall.
Strict Baptist, by 1937, secular,
TQ846857.
Congregational, 1893, 1909,
Congregational, TQ843860.
Decorated Gothic; by Smee and
Houchin.

Primitive Methodist, by 1908, secular, TQ842863.

Wesleyan Methodist, 1811, 1878, 1932, Methodist, TQ836858.

Wesleyan Methodist, 1877, 1911, Methodist, TQ838878.

Wesleyan Methodist, 1897, 1903, Methodist, TQ841860.

Wesleyan Methodist, 1927, 1956, Methodist, TQ824866. The earlier Gothic building is now the Hall.

Peculiar People, 1923, secular, TQ841863. Now in community use.

Society of Friends, 1936 (adopted), Society of Friends, TQ849862.

Prittlewell
Strict Baptist, 1893, Baptist (Grace), TQ878867.

Baptist, 1940, Baptist, TQ869876.

Congregational, 1900, United Reformed, TQ875864. Gothic, by Burles and Harris.

Peculiar People, 1904, religious, TQ876866.

Shoebury & Thorpe Bay
Baptist, 1927, 1984, Baptist, TQ927850. Coloured glass in the clerestory windows with a Biblical theme. The baptistry is visible below the communion table.

Primitive Methodist, 1899, Methodist, TQ930848.

*Free Church/Wesleyan Methodist, 1921, 1960, 1995, Methodist, TQ914851. Swedish portal frames used in its construction.

Peculiar People, 1932, religious, TQ928850.

Southchurch
Congregational, 1894, 1907, United Reformed, TQ896850.

Wesleyan Methodist, 1923, 1955, Methodist, TQ902866. The first, Gothic, building continues in secular use.

Southend
Particular Baptist, 1878, 1885, 1900, Baptist, TQ874855. Decorated Gothic. The second building continues in religious use.

Particular Baptist, 1883, 1902, 1961, Baptist, TQ881853.

Baptist, 1903, 1913, Baptist, TQ894895. Gothic with tower.

Baptist, 1932, c1980, Baptist, TQ891865. The earlier building is still in use as a Hall.

Independent, 1806, 1865, United Reformed, TQ880854. Gothic with tower and rose window; by W. Allen Dixon.

Congregational, 1897, 1925, United Reformed, TQ887864.

Primitive Methodist, 1907, Methodist, TQ889862.

Peculiar People, 1877, 1968, religious, TQ883860.

Peculiar People, 1902, religious, TQ883862.

Unitarian, 1898, 1977, Unitarian, TQ886856.

Westcliff
Baptist, 1896, 1914, Baptist, TQ863862. By G.Baines.

Congregational, 1897, United Reformed, TQ853860. Gothic.

*Congregational, 1910, 1924 United Reformed, TQ862858. Decorated Gothic by G.Baines, to match the earlier building by Burles and Harris. [F]

Congregational, 1961, United Reformed, TQ852877.

United Methodist Free Church, 1901, Methodist, TQ868860. Redesigned by K.Cheeseman.

Wesleyan Methodist, 1871, Methodist, TQ876854. Gothic by E. Hoole.

Wesleyan Methodist, c1900, religious, TQ872865.

Wesleyan Methodist, 1911, 1930, Methodist, TQ854866. Gothic.

SOUTHMINSTER
Particular Baptist, 1860, Baptist, TQ956995.

Independent, 1830, 1845, 1953, United Reformed, TQ959998.

STAMBOURNE
Presbyterian/Independent, 1717, 1969, Congregational, TL708389.

STANFORD-LE-HOPE
Wesleyan Methodist, 1869, Methodist, TQ685824.

Wesleyan Methodist, 1900, Methodist, TQ673796.

Peculiar People, 1870, 1924, religious, TQ684827.

STANSTED MOUNTFITCHET
*Independent, 1698, 1864, United Reformed, TL513249. Lombardic, by J. Carvell.

Primitive Methodist, c1880, secular, TL512254.

Society of Friends, 1704, 1967, Society of Friends, TL510250.

STEBBING
Independent, 1719, 1793, 1877, secular, TL660242. Now used as offices.

Primitive Methodist, 1864, empty, TL654254

*Society of Friends, 1674, secular, TL662241. Pyramid roof. The building is in community use. [G]

STEEPLE
*Congregational, 1857, Congregational, TL938030.

Peculiar People, 1877, secular, TL930026. Now a house.

STEEPLE BUMPSTEAD
Congregational, c1800, 1883, Congregational, TL680411. Gothic, by G. Bell.

STOCK
Congregational, 1812, 1889, Baptist, TQ689988.

TAKELEY
Congregational, 1808, 1902, Congregational, TL557211.

TENDRING
Wesleyan Methodist, 1835, 1869, secular, TM140258. Now a house.

TERLING
*Independent, 1714 (adopted), 1752, United Reformed, TL772148. Square with hipped roof.

THAXTED
Particular Baptist, 1813, 1833, Baptist, TL612307.

Independent, 1705, 1733, United Reformed, TL608309. Pediment and triple arched entrance.

Society of Friends, by 1684, by 1702, secular, TL613307.

THEYDON BOIS
*Baptist, 1894, 1962, Baptist, TQ449990.

THORPE-LE-SOKEN
✲Particular Baptist, 1802, Baptist, TM179223. Square with hipped roof.
Primitive Methodist, 1867, Methodist, TM180223.

THORRINGTON
Wesleyan Methodist, 1823, 1905, Methodist, TM095201.

THUNDERSLEY
Congregational, 1912, 1960, Congregational, TQ786880.
Wesleyan Methodist, 1924, 1993, Methodist, TQ770885.

TILBURY
Wesleyan Methodist, 1928, 1966, TQ642762. Polygonal with spire; by K. Cheeseman.

TILLINGHAM
Congregational, 1867, Congregational, TL992035.
✲Peculiar People, 1897, Peculiar People, TL993034.

TIPTREE
Independent, 1750, 1864, United Reformed, TL902160. Early English by F. Barnes.

TOLLESBURY
Presbyterian/Independent, by 1715, c1803, 1864, Congregational, TL956105. By C. Pertwee.

TOLLESHUNT D'ARCY
Congregational, 1881, 1888, United Reformed, TL930120. Decorative brickwork and window with six-pointed star.

TOLLESHUNT MAJOR
Congregational, 1859, secular, TL898111. Now a workshop.

TOPPESFIELD
Congregational, by 1830, 1881, Congregational, TL737373. The earlier building is now the Hall.

TOTHAM, GREAT
1830, 1871, United Reformed, TL868130. The earlier building is now the Hall. Decorative use of white brick.

TOTHAM, LITTLE
Peculiar People, 1890, religious, TL888119.

WAKERING, GREAT
Congregational, 1822, 1889, United Reformed, TQ946875.
Primitive Methodist, 1859, 1906, Methodist, TQ940874. Gothic.
Peculiar People, 1867, 1891, religious, TQ942875. [K]

WALTHAM, LITTLE
Independent, 1803, United Reformed, TL708128.
Congregational, 1872, secular, TL714153.

WALTHAM ABBEY
Particular Baptist, 1729, 1836, Baptist, TL380005. Early English, Y-mullioned windows.
✲Wesleyan Methodist, 1903, 1975, Methodist, TL387005. The earlier building is still in religious use.

WALTON-ON-THE-NAZE
Baptist, 1925 (adopted), Baptist, TM258227.
Baptist, 1992, Baptist, TM240212.
Congregational, 1836, 1853, 1878, Methodist & United Reformed, TM253216. Gothic. [H]
Primitive Methodist, 1875, empty, TM253216. [h]
Society of Friends, 1871, religious, TM251216.

WEELEY
Primitive Methodist, 1858, empty, TM154207.
✲Wesleyan Methodist, 1835, 1870, Methodist, TM146222.

WENDENS AMBO
Independent, 1751, 1851, secular, TL514365. Now a house.

WETHERSFIELD
Presbyterian/Independent, 1707, United Reformed, TL711313. The brickwork shows the later enlargement.
Congregational, 1861, Congregational, TL742290.

WICKFORD
Baptist, 1926, Baptist, TQ765930.
Methodist & United Reformed, 1974, Methodist & United Reformed, TQ746933. Polygonal with spire. [I]

Peculiar People, 1912, religious, TQ746931.

WITHAM
Strict and Particular Baptist, 1828,1846, secular, TL821144. Now a house.
Independent, 1715, 1840, United Reformed, TL820144. Pilasters and pediment.
Wesleyan Methodist, 1864, 1961, Methodist, TL819144. The earlier Gothic building is used as a Hall.
Peculiar People, 1858, 1874,1932, religious, TL817146.
Society of Friends, c1809, secular, TL823144. Now a Masonic Hall.

WIVENHOE
Presbyterian,/Independent, by 1719, 1805, 1846, 1962, Congregational, TM038219. The 1846 building, in classical style by J. Fenton, is still in use as flats. The present building by L. & D. Kemble.
Wesleyan Methodist, 1871, 1901, Methodist, TM039221.

WIX
Wesleyan Methodist, 1842, empty, TM168285. [j]
Methodist, 1935, Methodist, TM160283. [J]

WOODHAM FERRERS
Independent, 1843, 1884, Congregational, TQ796001.

WOODHAM FERRERS, SOUTH
Baptist, 1926, religious, TQ808975.
✲Methodist & Anglican & Roman Catholic, 1982, Methodist & Anglican & Roman Catholic, TQ812973.

WOODHAM WALTER
Congregational, 1881, secular, TL809069. Now a shop.

WRABNESS
Wesleyan Methodist, 1845, 1908, empty, TM175307.

WRITTLE
Independent, 1815, 1885, United Reformed, TL676063.

YELDHAM, GREAT
Particular Baptist, 1867, Baptist, TL761378.

SECTION ONE B

Buildings which still stand in the London Boroughs which used to be part of Essex.

LONDON BOROUGH OF BARKING AND DAGENHAM

BARKING

Particular Baptist, 1851, 1893, Baptist, TQ441843. Grecian Renaissance.

Baptist, 1935, Baptist, TQ454850.

Independent, 1785, c1825, 1863, 1929, United Reformed, TQ455846. The 1863 building by W.P. Poulton, the 1929 by J.S. Broadbent.

Wesleyan Methodist, 1797, 1869, 1928, 1958, Methodist, TQ442841.

Peculiar People, 1898 (adopted), 1962, religious, TQ455830.

Society of Friends, 1673 (adopted), 1758, 1908, religious, TQ440840. By D.J. Dawson

CHADWELL HEATH

Particular Baptist, by 1829, 1844, 1860, 1904, Baptist, TQ480879. Gothic.

Baptist, 1944, Baptist, TQ480890.

Baptist, 1957, Baptist, TQ477896. By J.J.M. Smith.

Congregational, 1885, 1910, United Reformed, TQ483884. Latin cross plan, by T.S. Leld. The first chapel, by E.C. Allam, is now the Hall.

DAGENHAM

Baptist, 1928, Baptist, TQ483843.

*Baptist, 1929,1964, Baptist, TQ483866. The earlier building used as a Hall.

Baptist, 1932, Baptist, TQ480858. By S.J. Haines.

Baptist, 1938, Baptist, TQ498858.

Congregational, 1931, 1987, Congregational, TQ488855. The earlier building by J.S. Broadbent.

United Methodist Free Church, 1875, 1971, Methodist, TQ490870. By J.R. Atkinson. [BB]

Wesleyan Methodist, 1854, 1888, 1962, Methodist, TQ503845.

Wesleyan Methodist, 1925, 1930, 1982, Methodist, TQ491841.

Methodist, 1936, secular, TQ473851. Now used by the Health Authority.

LONDON BOROUGH OF HAVERING

HORNCHURCH

Baptist, 1914, 1933, Baptist, TQ539894.

Baptist, 1938, 1963, Baptist, TQ525854.

Independent/Baptist, 1859, 1882, 1986, Baptist, TQ539872. Shops on the ground floor.

Congregational, 1909, United Reformed, TQ542882.

Wesleyan Methodist, 1926, 1958, Methodist, TQ531889.

Methodist, 1933, 1958, Methodist, TQ536872.

RAINHAM

*Wesleyan Methodist, 1929, 1959, Methodist, TQ525819. The earlier building, by J.S. Broadbent, is now the Hall.

Methodist, 1957, 1986, Methodist, TQ521847.

ROMFORD

Particular Baptist, 1840, 1847, Baptist, TQ508884. Pilasters and broken pediment.

Strict Baptist, c1927, 1936, 1953, Strict Baptist, TQ521884.

Baptist, c1930, Baptist, TQ559915.

Baptist, 1934, Baptist, TQ515891.

Baptist, 1954, Baptist, TQ536926.

Baptist, 1961, Baptist, TQ502913.

Independent, 1700, 1717, 1823, [CC], 1877, 1883, 1965, United Reformed, TQ517889. The 1876 building by E.C. Allam.

Congregational, 1962, United Reformed, TQ530914.

Primitive Methodist, 1875, 1950, secular, TQ517886. The first building by E.C. Allam; the second by Evans, Crowe, Thompson and Whitehead, now in community use.

*Wesleyan Methodist, 1827, 1887, Methodist, TQ510888. Early English.

United Methodist, 1929, 1962, TQ547907. The earlier building is now the Hall.

Methodist, 1954, Methodist, TQ500916. By Baines and Syborn.

*Methodist, 1957, 1974, Methodist, TQ509911.

Society of Friends, 1944 (adopted), 1961, Society of Friends, TQ525897. By N. Frith.

UPMINSTER

*Baptist, 1935, 1959, Baptist, TQ560862. The earlier building is now the Hall.

Baptist, 1957, Baptist, TQ571882.

Independent, 1800, 1910, United Reformed, TQ560867. Gothic, by T. Stevens. The earlier building, refronted in classical style, is being restored.

Congregational, 1915, secular, TQ556847.

Wesleyan Methodist, 1910, 1923, Methodist, TQ562869.

The Wesleyan Methodist chapel at Romford built in 1887.

LONDON BOROUGH OF NEWHAM

LONDON E16
Baptist, 1927, Baptist, TQ410815.

Methodist, 1960, Methodist, TQ402815. Replacing four chapels. [L]

Peculiar People, 1873, 1959, religious, TQ397819.

FOREST GATE
Particular Baptist, 1881, Baptist and secular, TQ407850. The chapel, by Wallis Chapman, with Arts and Crafts influence, is in secular use; the original Hall is now used for worship.

Particular Baptist, 1886, secular, TQ404839. Now in community use.

Strict Baptist, 1906, Baptist (Grace), TQ414845.

Strict Baptist, 1921, secular, TQ412855. Now a house.

Congregational, 1831, 1856, 1884, religious, TQ407854. By F.J. Sturdy, with classical features. The first building is now a shop.

Congregational, 1880, 1883, secular, TQ402849. Gothic, flint with brick dressing, by Lewis Banks. The earlier building became the Hall.

Congregational, 1890, 1895, 1926, secular, TQ416842. Now a school.

Primitive Methodist, 1882, secular, TQ403857. By W. Dartnell. Now in community use. [m]

Primitive Methodist, 1892, secular, TQ404844. [m]

Wesleyan Methodist, 1878, 1882, 1961, Methodist, TQ405851. Replacing five previous chapels. [M]

Unitarian, 1893, religious, TQ405846.

EAST HAM
Baptist, 1895, 1900, Baptist, TQ419841.

Baptist, 1928, Baptist, TQ430830.

Congregational, 1890, 1901, 1957, Congregational &

Methodist, TQ424837. The 1901 building by Mould and Porritt. [N]

Primitive Methodist, 1885, Methodist, TQ428828. Pediment and pilasters.

Primitive Methodist, 1886, religious, TQ416835.

*Primitive Methodist, 1889, religious, TQ414840.

Presbyterian (CoE), 1903, secular, TQ423844. Gothic, by J. Willis. Now in community use. [O]

Interdenominational, 1987, Interdenominational, TQ427816.

MANOR PARK
Particular Baptist, 1889, 1895, 1900, 1905, 1957, Baptist, TQ429859. The 1905 building has gone leaving the later Youth Hall as the chapel.

Particular Baptist, 1893 (adopted), 1898, 1906, Baptist, TQ421851. Gothic with tower.

Strict Baptist, 1907, secular, TQ421854. Now in community use.

Baptist, c1900, religious, TQ432854.

Congregational, c1860 (adopted), 1890, religious, TQ419856.

Congregational, 1897, 1904, United Reformed and secular, TQ421849. Gothic with tower, by G. Baines. Converted to a small chapel and workshops.

Primitive Methodist, 1901, religious, TQ426858. [p]

United Methodist, 1880, 1891, 1964, Methodist, TQ422856. [P]

United Methodist, 1894, secular, TQ422844. Now used by a firm of Solicitors.

PLAISTOW
*Particular Baptist, 1863, 1876, 1921, Baptist, TQ405824. Byzantine influence, by W. Hayne. The 1876 building is still in religious use.

Congregational, 1886, 1892, 1949, 1954, United Reformed, TQ411830. [Q]

Congregational, 1959, United Reformed, TQ415826.

United Methodist, 1868, 1902, religious, TQ407836. [R]

Wesleyan Methodist (Welsh), 1915, religious, TQ406819.

STRATFORD
Particular Baptist, 1854, Baptist, TQ391848. Gothic. [S]

Particular Baptist, 1885, 1953, Baptist, TQ384853.

Strict and Particular Baptist, 1844, 1903, Baptist (Grace), TQ392838.

Strict and Particular Baptist, c1880, 1884, Baptist (Grace), TQ394854.

Presbyterian/Independent, c1700, 1776, United Reformed, TQ394842. Extended and altered.

Methodist, 1934 (adopted), 1964, Methodist, TQ390841.

Methodist, 1945 (adopted), Methodist, TQ389848.

Wesleyan Association/Unitarian, 1838, 1869, Unitarian, TQ390842.

LONDON BOROUGH OF REDBRIDGE

CHIGWELL
Methodist, 1961, 1989, Methodist, TQ456924.

ILFORD
Particular Baptist, 1801, 1882, 1907, Baptist, TQ444866. Gothic with tower and spire, by G. Baines.

Strict and Particular Baptist, c1836, 1898, 1932, 1965, religious, TQ435868.

Baptist, 1908, 1926, Baptist, TQ438858.

Baptist, 1920, 1959, Baptist, TQ464871. By E.W. Banfield.

Baptist, 1929, Baptist, TQ439884. By W. Hayne.

Baptist, 1932, Baptist, TQ418885. By Baines (son).

Baptist, 1938, Baptist, TQ427904.

Baptist, 1948, 1963, Baptist, TQ449916. By A.E. Edwards.

Congregational, 1894, 1900, 1961, United Reformed, TQ440865. The 1900 building in late Gothic by Mould, the 1961 building by Tooley Foster.

Congregational, 1895, 1906, secular, TQ433869. Gothic, by G. Baines. Now used as offices. [t]

Congregational, 1903, 1927, United Reformed, TQ464870. Gothic; curved pews and radial aisles but pulpit removed.

Congregational, 1907, 1936, Baptist & United Reformed, TQ454878. The earlier building is now the Hall. [U]

Congregational, 1931, United Reformed, TQ431885. By Smee and Houchin. [T]

Primitive Methodist, 1900, 1966, Methodist, TQ463878.

United Methodist, 1867, 1902, 1961, Methodist, TQ437860. The second building by F. W. Dixon in perpendicular style. [V]

United Methodist, 1905, Methodist, TQ455870. Gothic, by G. Baines.

United Methodist, 1928, Methodist, TQ423883. Gothic, Latin cross plan. Oak panelled inside.

Wesleyan Methodist, 1847, 1937, 1959. Methodist, TQ440900. The second chapel is now the Hall.

Wesleyan Methodist, 1904, religious, TQ460874. Gothic.

Wesleyan Methodist, 1928, Methodist, TQ437889.

Wesleyan Methodist, 1900, 1933, 1977, Methodist, TQ452885. The second building is now the Hall while the first is used by Education.

Society of Friends, 1906, 1927, Society of Friends, TQ439861. By C. Culpin.

Unitarian, 1908, religious, TQ446867. Decorated Gothic.

LEYTONSTONE

Baptist, 1893, Baptist, TQ404888.

Congregational, 1866 (adopted), United Reformed, TQ405886. Decorated Gothic; an Anglican building moved from Kings Cross.

United Methodist Free Church, 1865, 1875, Methodist, TQ405882. Gothic, by F. Boreham.

Wesleyan Methodist, 1876,

Methodist, TQ404888. Gothic, by J.T. Bressey.

Society of Friends, 1673, 1870 (adopted), 1968, Society of Friends, TQ400875. By N. Frith.

MANOR PARK

Baptist, 1909, Baptist, TQ412868. Tower and spire.

WOODFORD GREEN

Baptist, 1957, 1963, Baptist, TQ418912. By D. Hall, who also carved the wooden pattern on the facade. The earlier building is now the Hall.

Congregational, c1870, 1900, 1986, United Reformed, TQ414918. The 1900 building in Gothic style was by F. Boreham.

Congregational, 1890, 1964, United Reformed, TQ428921.

Wesleyan Reformers/Free Methodist, c1852, 1869, 1903, United Reformed, TQ400922. Arts and Crafts, and Byzantine influence, by Harrison Townsend. The second building by R. Plumbe. [W]

WOODFORD SOUTH

Particular Baptist, 1883, 1895, Baptist, TQ406899. Decorated Gothic. The earlier building is now the Hall.

Wesleyan Methodist, 1876, Methodist, TQ399908.

LONDON BOROUGH OF WALTHAM FOREST

CHINGFORD

Strict Baptist, 1934, 1953, Baptist (Grace), TQ386941. By A.R. Dannatt.

Baptist, 1938, 1961, Baptist, TQ373934. The earlier building is now the Hall.

Congregational, 1888, 1890, 1909, United Reformed, TQ388946. Gothic with tower and spire, by J.D. and S.J. Mould.

*Congregational, 1905, 1954, Congregational, TQ372923. Tower and decorative tile doorway.

Congregational & United Methodist, 1897, 1927, United Reformed, TQ386912.

United Methodist, 1902, 1903,

Methodist, TQ384913. Gothic, by G. Baines and Son.

Weslyan Methodist, 1862, 1947, Methodist & Anglican, TQ390931.

Weslyan Methodist, 1905, 1927, Methodist, TQ388943. Gothic, by G. Baines and Son.

Weslyan Methodist, 1909, 1986, Methodist, TQ389919.

Wesleyan Methodist, 1931, 1935, Methodist, TQ374927. The earlier chapel is now the Hall.

FOREST GATE

Congregational, 1888, religious, TQ395859. An iron building.

LEYTON

Particular Baptist, 1869-79, secular, TQ378867.

Particular Baptist, 1875, Baptist, TQ375874.

Congregational, 1874, 1984, United Reformed, TQ379868. The earlier building is still in secular use. By C. Lake and D. Pearce.

*Congregational, 1885, 1891, 1899, religious, TQ385860. By Morley Horder, influenced by Mackintosh of Glasgow.

Primitive Methodist, 1883, 1892, 1974, Methodist, TQ381864. By J. Steed. [X]

LEYTONSTONE

Particular Baptist, 1878, 1991, Baptist & United Reformed, TQ389876. The earlier building by L. Cubitt. [Y]

Particular Baptist, 1881, 1886, Baptist, TQ393857. By G Baines.

Baptist, 1902, 1925, 1957, religious, TQ392862. By J. Reeve Young.

Primitive Methodist/Strict Baptist, 1868, 1926, Baptist (Grace), TQ382873.

Primitive Methodist, 1901, religious, TQ393878. By Clark Hallam.

United Methodist, 1887, Methodist, TQ386866.

Wesleyan Methodist, 1876, 1880, 1972, Methodist, TQ394871.

LEYTONSTONE continued
✽Wesleyan Methodist, 1887, 1898, 1992, Methodist, TQ397861. By K. Cheeseman.
Presbyterian (CoW), 1933 (adopted), 1958, Presbyterian (CoW), TQ396876.

WALTHAMSTOW
Old Baptist, 1907, religious, TQ385891. Venetian window.
Old Baptist, 1910, Old Baptist, TQ380908.
Particular Baptist, 1875, 1880, 1913, Baptist, TQ375888. Gothic. The second building by Sears is still in religious use.
Strict and Particular Baptist, 1874, 1914, 1984, Baptist (Grace), TQ375893. The chapel is incorporated in a block of flats.
Baptist, 1892, secular, TQ362894.

Baptist, 1898, 1932, Baptist, TQ360890.
Baptist, 1904, religious, TQ363900. By E. Stones.
Baptist, 1905, 1911, Baptist, TQ379905.
Baptist, 1906, 1914, 1949, Baptist, TQ371895.
Baptist, 1917, Baptist, TQ381914.
Congregational, 1861, 1864, 1869, United Reformed, TQ376888. Gothic, by Sutton. [EE]
Union (Baptist & Congregational), 1811, 1845, 1854, 1955, United Reformed, TQ383894. By E. Snaith.
Calvinistic Methodist, 1933 (adopted), religious, TQ376892.
United Methodist, 1889, 1892, Methodist, TQ365881. 'Lighthouse', with tower;

remodelled interior by K. Cheeseman, with worship area upstairs.
United Methodist, 1897, 1900, 1976, Methodist, TQ384889. The second, Gothic, building by G. Baines, the third by K. Cheeseman.
United Methodist, 1903, 1912, religious, TQ371898.
United Methodist, 1908, 1930, 1939, Methodist, TQ374906. The second chapel by G. Baines and Son.
Welsh Calvinistic Methodist, by 1919, secular, TQ377885. Now a shop.
Society of Friends, 1903, 1997 (adopted), Society of Friends, TQ371895.
Unitarian, 1939, religious, TQ368890.

SECTION TWO A

Chapels which have been demolished and not replaced in present-day Essex.

ABBERTON
Wesleyan Methodist, 1816; (1951), TM003187.
ALTHORNE
Particular Baptist, 1834; after 1932.
ARKESDEN
Independent, 1843; (1851).
AVELEY
Primitive Methodist, 1851; (1855).
BARDFIELD, GREAT
Independent, (1863).
BASILDON
Baptist, 1898.
Baptist, 1932; (1965).
Congregational, 1880; 1958, TQ738882.
BELCHAM OTTEN
Baptist/Congregational, 1886; (1908), TL801416.
BERGHOLT, WEST
Wesleyan Methodist, 1820; 1866, TL967276.
BILLERICAY
Strict and Particular Baptist/Congregational, 1874; 1987, TQ684934.

BOREHAM
Congregational, 1867; 1972, TL760103.
BRADFIELD
Primitive Methodist, 1840, 1870; (1937), TM137298.
BRADWELL-NEXT-THE-SEA
Primitive Methodist, 1863; (1964), TL995078.
BRAINTREE
Strict and Particular Baptist, 1846, 1865, by 1877; 1975, TL764230.
Wesleyan Methodist, 1818, 1868; 1988, TL755231. Gothic. [a]
Society of Friends, 1706, 1863; 1956, TL755232.
BRENTWOOD
General Baptist, by 1715.
Strict and Particular Baptist, 1855; (1908)
Primitive Methodist, 1847; by 1850, TQ592929.
BRIGHTLINGSEA
Particular Baptist, 1838; by 1851, TM090168.
Free Methodist/Wesleyan Reform, 1860; 1936, TM086168.

Primitive Methodist, 1902; 1945, TM084170.
BURNHAM-ON-CROUCH
Strict and Particular Baptist, 1751, 1806; (1932), TQ954955.
Primitive Methodist, 1902; 1925.
Wesleyan Methodist, 1842; TQ952957.
BUCKHURST HILL
Wesleyan Methodist, 1886; 1980, TQ414937.
CHELMSFORD
Presbyterian, 1688, after 1759, 1859; 1970, cTL714062. The 1859 chapel by Poulton and Woodman.[c]
Independent, c1740, 1786, 1839; 1970, cTL7070654. The 1839 chapel was classical, by Fenton. [c]
Congregational, 1860; (1954), TL701050.
Congregational, 1861; 1989, TL723079.
Congregational, 1861; 1943, TL705072. Gothic.
Presbyterian (CoS), 1836; by 1851, TL709063.

Barnes' drawing of his proposed design for the Lion Walk Congregational chapel, Colchester, in 1863.

Reproduced by courtesy of Essex Record Office.

Unitarian, (1878); 1913, TL708070.
CHESTERFORD, LITTLE
Wesleyan Methodist, 1872; (1937), TL518419.
CLACTON, GREAT
Primitive Methodist, 1863; (1937), TM173157.
CLAVERING
Particular Baptist, (1774).
COLCHESTER
Seventh Day Baptist, c1650; (1773).
General Baptist; by 1755.
Baptist, 1900; 1910, TL992248.
Congregational, 1845, 1851; 1938, cTM013246.
Primitive Methodist/Wesleyan Methodist, 1824; 1897, TM003248.
Primitive Methodist, 1895; by 1921, TL989279.
Wesleyan Methodist, 1869; 1956, TM012247.
Presbyterian, 1693; 1823, TL996254.
COLNE ENGAINE
Primitive Methodist, (1876); TL849304.

COLNE, WAKES
Peculiar People, c1920; c1958, TL896308.
COLNE, WHITE
Particular Baptist, 1846; by 1870.
CRESSING
Independent, 1847; by 1878.
Peculiar People, 1908; (1922), TL788203.
DANBURY
Peculiar People, 1872; 1956, TL796028.
Presbyterian, 1672; (1900), TL788053.
DEBDEN
General Baptist, (1851).
DEDHAM
General Baptist.
DOVERCOURT
Congregational, 1908; 1988, TM254314. Gothic, by H.H. Packer. [e]
Primitive Methodist, 1880, 1895; 1939, TM259318.
DUNMOW
Particular Baptist, 1823; c1970, TL628221. A square chapel.
EASTER, HIGH
Particular Baptist, (1715).
EASTON, GREAT
Independent, 1821, 1882; 1970, TL618259.
Primitive Methodist, 1837; (1851), TL615239.
ELMDON
Primitive Methodist, 1845; by 1896, TL4639.
ELMSTEAD
Primitive Methodist, 1904; by 1970, TM063224.
Wesleyan Reform, (1851); TM063224.
ELSENHAM
Society of Friends, 1882; 1985, TL536262.
EPPING
Particular Baptist, 1863, 1893; (1979), TL457023.
FELSTEAD
Society of Friends, 1687, 1764; c1940, TL694207. [g]
FINCHINGFIELD
Particular (later Strict) Baptist, 1849; (1932).

FOBBING
Wesleyan Methodist, 1887; 1954, TQ717840.
FOULNESS
Peculiar People. [k]
GOLDHANGER
Particular Baptist, (1878).
GRAYS
Strict and Particular Baptist, 1878; (1983), TQ620777.
Primitive Methodist, 1870; 1948, TQ615776.
Wesleyan Methodist/Wesleyan Reform, 1847, 1873; 1932, TQ618776.
Wesleyan Methodist, 1876; 1978, TQ633788.
Wesleyan Methodist, 1884; 1985, TQ613780.
Society of Friends, 1906 (adopted); 1953.
HALSTEAD
Congregational, 1833; 1946, TL812306. Gothic, Early English.
Unitarian, 1857; 1958, TL813305.
HARLOW
Wesleyan Methodist, 1887; 1963, TL447111.
HARWICH
Presbyterian/Independent, by 1715, 1800; 1945, TM260325.
Wesleyan Methodist, 1829; 1969, TM260326.
Society of Friends, 1709, 1786; 1800, TM260325.
HEDINGHAM, CASTLE
Independent, 1853; (1860).
HEDINGHAM, SIBLE
Primitive Methodist, 1867; by 1896.
HEMPSTEAD
Independent, 1855; TL634379.
HORNDON-ON-THE-HILL
Particular Baptist, 1835; (1851).
KIRBY
Wesleyan Methodist, 1825; 1947, TM211210. A square chapel.
LAMARSH
Particular Baptist, 1830; 1979, TL891356.

LANGHAM
  Particular Baptist, 1754; 1941,
  TM029335.
LAYER BRETON
  Society of Friends, 1827; 1984,
  TL946182.
LAYER-DE-LA-HAYE
  Primitive Methodist, 1864;
  1969, TL978201.
LEIGHS, GREAT
  Particular Baptist, 1854; 1890,
  TL739160.
LITTLEBURY
  Primitive Methodist, c1900
  (adopted); TL517396.
MALDON
  Strict and Particular Baptist,
  1835,1861; (1932), TL857078.
MANNINGTREE
  Society of Friends, by 1712; 1795.
MANUDEN
  Independent, 1826; (1922).
MAPLESTEAD, LITTLE
  Independent, 1817, 1841; 1978,
  TL833341.
MATCHING GREEN
  Particular Baptist, 1885, 1950;
  1990, TL534112.
MERSEA, EAST
  General Baptist, 1731, 1798;
  1863.
MESSING   Congregational,
  1864; 1930.
MOUNTNESSING
  Congregational, 1881, 1949;
  1968, TQ630977.
NEWPORT
  Independent, by 1715, 1778,
  1879; 1978, TL520337. By C.
  Pertwee.
NORTH WEALD BASSETT
  Independent, 1826; 1874,
  cTL509055.
  Wesleyan Methodist, 1883;
  1939, TL470045.
NORTON MANDERVILLE
  Congregational, 1876; 1969,
  TL601040. An iron building.
  Wesleyan Methodist, (1886).
OAKLEY, GREAT
  Particular Baptist, 1828; 1843,
  TM194275.

Primitive Methodist, 1850;
  (1937), TM167266.
  Society of Friends; by 1748; 1784
ORSETT
  Primitive Methodist, 1857; by
  1935, TQ635812.
PELDON
  Wesleyan Methodist, 1893;
  1970, TL987163.
QUENDON
  Independent, 1819, 1840; 1968,
  TL510300.
RADWINTER
  Independent, 1850; (1863).
  Primitive Methodist, 1851.
RAMSDEN BELLHOUSE
  Peculiar People, 1883; by 1979,
  TQ714960.
ROCHFORD
  Particular Baptist, 1839; (1932).
  Strict Baptist, 1872; by 1890.
  Peculiar People, 1850, 1904,
  1969; c1990, TQ880905.
RODING, ABBESS
  Presbyterian, 1729; 1890,
  TL561118.
RODING, LEADEN
  Congregational, 1870; 1980,
  TL595134.
ROYDON
  Particular Baptist, 1798; (1834).
  Congregational, 1869, 1891;
  1970, TL424070.
SALING
  Society of Friends, 1675; 1799.
SHEERING
  Wesleyan Methodist, 1885;
  (1922), TL508139.
SOUTHEND
  Baptist, 1899; 1954,
  cTQ870858.
  Baptist, (1921); TQ915852.
  Free Methodist, 1866; (1900),
  cTQ891849.
  Primitive Methodist, 1906;
  (1968), TQ866865.
  Wesleyan Methodist, 1893;
  1964, TQ939849.
  Wesleyan Methodist, 1898,
  1908; 1987, TQ889855.
  Methodist, (1937); TQ912862.

Presbyterian (CoE), 1898; 1982,
  TQ876857. [f]
STAMBRIDGE, GREAT
  Baptist, (1922); 1994, TQ899917.
STANFORD RIVERS
  Congregational, 1820; 1927,
  TL540003. Classical.
STANSTED MOUNTFITCHET
  Independent, 1822; 1844.
STISTED
  Independent, 1835; 1980,
  TL800247.
TERLING
  Baptist, (1715); TL772148.
  Society of Friends; by 1799,
  cTL7717.
TEY, GREAT
  Congregational, 1879; 1957,
  TL897259.
TEY, MARKS
  Particular Baptist, 1824, c1900;
  (1922), TL913234.
THUNDERSLEY
  Baptist, 1847,1874; by 1932.
THURROCK, WEST
  Primitive Methodist, 1876;
  1903, TQ591777.
  Wesleyan Methodist, 1791; 1863.
TILBURY
  General Baptist.
TILLINGHAM
  Particular Baptist, 1830; 1892,
  TL994037.
  Primitive Methodist, 1811
  (adopted); (1932), TL992034.
TOLLESHUNT KNIGHTS
  Congregational, 1864; (1920),
  TL918144. An iron building.
TOTHAM, GREAT
  Wesleyan Methodist, 1851; by
  1964, TL869133.
WALDEN, LITTLE
  Congregational, 1851; 1929,
  TL546415.
WALTHAM ABBEY
  Particular Baptist, 1824, 1868,
  1879; 1921, TL381004.
  Strict and Particular Baptist,
  1845; (1910), TL381006.
  Wesleyan Methodist, 1876;
  (1937), TQ395973.
  Wesleyan Methodist, by 1931;
  (1968), TQ381975.

Society of Friends, 1698; 1840, cTL005383.

WALTHAM, GREAT
Particular Baptist, 1872; by 1955, TL678167.
Congregational, 1844; by 1980, TL677167.
Primitive Methodist, 1860; 1980, TL697145.

WETHERSFIELD
Independent, c1740; c1756.

WICKFORD
Presbyterian/Independent, 1725,

1811, 1875; 1972, cTQ746934. Romanesque. [i]
Wesleyan Methodist, 1928; 1980. [i]

WICKHAM BISHOPS
Particular Baptist, 1843, (1867).

WICKHAM ST PAUL
Primitive Methodist, 1869; 1975, TL830364.

WIDDINGTON
Congregational, 1858; 1990, TL538316.

WIX
Primitive Methodist, 1880; 1935, TM148278. [j]

WORMINGFORD
Primitive Methodist, 1898; 1971, TL939316. An iron building.

WOODHAM FERRERS,
Peculiar People, 1862; c1960, TL796028.

WRITTLE
Wesleyan Methodist, after 1851, 1895; by 1935, TL667061.

SECTION TWO B
Chapels which have been demolished and not replaced in London Boroughs which used to be part of Essex.

LONDON BOROUGH OF BARKING AND DAGENHAM
BARKING
Primitive Methodist, by 1861; by 1933, TQ440844.
CHADWELL HEATH
Independent/Wesleyan Methodist, 1821, 1962; by 1980, TQ484902.
DAGENHAM
Wesleyan Methodist/Wesleyan Reform, by 1829; 1875, TQ492868. [bb]
Wesleyan Methodist/Wesleyan Reform, 1846; 1875, TQ502845. [bb]
Wesleyan Methodist, 1925; by 1980, TQ474866. Gothic.

LONDON BOROUGH OF HAVERING
HORNCHURCH
Methodist, 1936; by 1980, TQ516872.
RAINHAM
General Baptist.
Wesleyan Methodist, 1834; 1848, TQ525819.
ROMFORD
Strict and Particular Baptist, 1850, 1871; TQ513890.
Baptist, 1910, 1928; 1993, TQ501887.
Independent, 1796; 1819. [cc]
Congregational/Particular Baptist, 1861; (1882), TQ536907.

Wesleyan Methodist, 1877; 1890, cTQ504907.
Methodist, 1953; by 1990.
Peculiar People, 1934; (1979), TQ517882.
Presbyterian, by 1715; 1819. [cc]
UPMINSTER
Congregational, 1850; 1940, TQ561898.

LONDON BOROUGH OF NEWHAM
LONDON E16
Particular Baptist, 1887; by 1972, TQ422801.
Strict and Particular Baptist, by 1870; 1917, TQ397812.
Baptist, 1899, 1952; 1982, TQ434810.
Baptist, 1903; 1939.
Congregational, 1860, 1868, 1949; 1959, TQ394816.
Union (Baptist & Congregational & Presbyterian), 1869; 1921, TQ399809.
Union (Baptist & Congregational), 1885; 1908, TQ412810.
Congregational, 1904; by 1945, TQ398818. An iron chapel.
Primitive Methodist, 1859, 1877; 1943, TQ397817. [l]
Primitive Methodist, 1880; by 1945, TQ434800.

Primitive Methodist, 1883, 1888; 1960, TQ404811. [l]
United Methodist, 1860, 1873; 1940, TQ397813. [l]
Wesleyan Methodist, 1862, 1868, 1887, 1948; 1960, TQ396817. [l]
Wesleyan Methodist, 1871, 1914; 1959, TQ425800.
Wesleyan Methodist (German), 1893; 1914, TQ396820.
Wesleyan Methodist, 1926; by 1935, TQ400808.
Peculiar People, 1893; by 1966, TQ418802.
Peculiar People, 1910; by 1956, TQ423801.
Presbyterian (CoE), 1872; 1941, TQ400809. [o]
Presbyterian (CoE), 1882; by 1945, TQ425801.
FOREST GATE
Primitive Methodist, 1903; (1912), TQ413846.
United Methodist, 1863, 1870; 1956, TQ402854. [m]
United Methodist, 1907; 1956, TQ412850. Gothic. [AA], [m]
Wesleyan Methodist, 1882, 1893; 1971, TQ411842. Gothic.
Society of Friends, 1906; by 1945, TQ410845.

EAST HAM

Congregational (Welsh), 1902; (1945), TQ425843. An iron chapel.

Primitive Methodist, 1901; by 1970, TQ434816.

Wesleyan Methodist, 1870, 1880, 1906; 1969, TQ427835. Central Hall by J. Gunton, in Queen Anne style. [n]

Wesleyan Methodist, 1891; 1904, TQ417836.

MANOR PARK

Strict Baptist, 1916; 1922, TQ426858.

Wesleyan Methodist, 1890, 1900; 1937, TQ422856. [p]

PLAISTOW

Independent Methodist & Baptist/Congregational, 1879, 1904 (adopted); 1909, TQ405833. The earlier building continued in religious use.

Union (Congregational & Baptist), 1807, 1860; 1941, TQ404828. [q]

Congregational, 1887; (1955), TQ409832.

Primitive Methodist, 1896; 1940, TQ400836.

Primitive Methodist, 1883; by 1945, TQ402826.

Wesleyan Methodist, 1870, 1880; 1941, TQ404831. [r]

Society of Friends, 1683, 1704, 1823; 1924, cTQ407833.

STRATFORD

Particular Baptist/Primitive Methodist, 1832, 1863; 1962, TQ386851.

Particular Baptist, 1842; 1854, TQ388841.

Particular Baptist, 1877; 1917, TQ385839. [s]

Congregational, 1866; 1948, TQ390847. Classical, by R. Plumbe.

Primitive Methodist, 1870 (adopted); 1906, cTQ388841.

Primitive Methodist, 1877.

Primitive Methodist, 1896; by 1922, TQ394833.

Wesleyan Association, 1838; (1857), cTQ387841.

Wesleyan Methodist, 1790, 1828 (adopted),1871; by 1945, TQ391847.

Wesleyan Reform/United Methodist, 1854, 1860; 1907, TQ387839. [aa]

Presbyterian (CoE), 1864, 1870; 1941, TQ392850. Gothic.

Presbyterian (CoW), 1894; 1940, TQ396845.

LONDON BOROUGH OF REDBRIDGE

BARKINGSIDE

Independent, 1818; (1870).

ILFORD

Particular Baptist, 1840; cTQ434862.

Particular Baptist, 1899, 1913; 1985, TQ464871. Gothic, by G. Baines. [u]

Congregational, 1906; 1941, TQ440852.

Congregational, 1918; 1940, TQ446886.

Primitive Methodist, 1897; 1936, TQ446866.

Primitive Methodist, 1904; 1934, cTQ456873.

Wesleyan Methodist, 1821; 1863, TQ435863.

Wesleyan Methodist, 1884, 1895; c1961, TQ437864. [v]

Wesleyan Methodist, 1904, 1914; 1970, TQ428875.

Presbyterian (CoE), 1896, 1903; c1970, TQ440863.

Presbyterian (CoE), 1905, 1912, 1950; c1972, TQ463870.

WOODFORD GREEN

Independent, 1794, 1803, 1837, 1873; 1944, TQ402918. Gothic. [w]

Primitive Methodist, 1888; 1913, TQ412918.

SOUTH WOODFORD

Baptist, 1897, 1906; 1920, TQ409906. An iron chapel.

Baptist, 1906; 1933, TQ409906. An iron chapel.

Congregational, 1872, 1885; 1983, TQ403903. By T. M. Arnold, in Gothic.

LONDON BOROUGH OF WALTHAM FOREST

LEYTON

Wesleyan Methodist, 1823, 1843, 1902; 1940, TQ381880. [x]

Wesleyan Methodist, 1877; 1969, TQ381876. Gothic.

LEYTONSTONE

Particular Baptist, 1883.

Congregational, 1827, 1873, 1877; 1986, TQ394871. By T. Lewis Banks, in Lombardic style. [y]

Presbyterian (CoE), 1888, 1893; 1939, TQ386876. Gothic.

WALTHAMSTOW

Particular Baptist, 1886; 1892, TQ368889.

Baptist, 1901; 1912, TQ368895.

Presbyterian/ Independent, 1695, 1740; 1835, TQ3789. [z]

Congregational, 1787; 1973, TQ367889. [Z], [dd]

Congregational, 1871; 1965, TQ3789. Gothic. [DD], [ee]

Congregational, 1900; 1946, TQ381905.

Primitive Methodist, 1879; 1972, TQ360904.

Primitive Methodist, 1880, 1923; 1937, TQ375910.

Primitive Methodist, 1882; 1917, TQ373897. Classical.

Wesleyan Methodist/Presbyterian, 1872, 1905; 1968, TQ379894.

Wesleyan Methodist, 1883, 1898; 1958, TQ361889.

Wesleyan Methodist, 1898; 1944, TQ374893.

Unitarian, 1897; 1938, TQ368890. An iron building.